Principles in Practice

The Principles in Practice imprint offers teachers concrete illustrations of effective classroom practices based in NCTE research briefs and policy statements. Each book discusses the research on a specific topic, links the research to an NCTE brief or policy statement, and then demonstrates how those principles come alive in practice: by showcasing actual classroom practices that demonstrate the policies in action; by talking about research in practical, teacher-friendly language; and by offering teachers possibilities for rethinking their own practices in light of the ideas presented in the books. Books within the imprint are grouped in strands, each strand focused on a significant topic of interest.

Adolescent Literacy Strand

Adolescent Literacy at Risk? The Impact of Standards (2009) Rebecca Bowers Sipe

Adolescents and Digital Literacies: Learning Alongside Our Students (2010) Sara Kajder

Adolescent Literacy and the Teaching of Reading: Lessons for Teachers of Literature (2010) Deborah Appleman

Writing in Today's Classrooms Strand

Writing in the Dialogical Classroom: Students and Teachers Responding to the Texts of Their Lives (2011) Bob Fecho

Becoming Writers in the Elementary Classroom: Visions and Decisions (2011) Katie Van Sluys

Writing Instruction in the Culturally Relevant Classroom (2011) Maisha T. Winn and Latrise P. Johnson

Literacy Assessment Strand

Our Better Judgment: Teacher Leadership for Writing Assessment (2012) Chris W. Gallagher and Eric D. Turley

Beyond Standardized Truth: Improving Teaching and Learning through Inquiry-Based Reading Assessment (2012) Scott Filkins

Reading Assessment: Artful Teachers, Successful Students (2013) Diane Stephens, editor

Literacies of the Disciplines Strand

Entering the Conversations: Practicing Literacy in the Disciplines (2014) Patricia Lambert Stock, Trace Schillinger, and Andrew Stock

Real-World Literacies: Disciplinary Teaching in the High School Classroom (2014) Heather Lattimer

Doing and Making Authentic Literacies (2014) Linda Denstaedt, Laura Jane Roop, and Stephen Best

Reading in Today's Classrooms Strand

Connected Reading: Teaching Adolescent Readers in a Digital World (2015) Kristen Hawley Turner and Troy Hicks

Digital Reading: What's Essential in Grades 3–8 (2015) William L. Bass II and Franki Sibberson

Teaching Reading with YA Literature: Complex Texts, Complex Lives (2016) Jennifer Buehler

Teaching English Language Learners Strand

Beyond "Teaching to the Test": Rethinking Accountability and Assessment for English Language Learners (2017) Betsy Gilliland and Shannon Pella

Community Literacies en Confianza: *Learning from Bilingual After-School Programs* (2017) Steven Alvarez

Understanding Language: Supporting ELL Students in Responsive ELA Classrooms (2017) Melinda J. McBee Orzulak

Understanding Language

Supporting ELL Students in Responsive ELA Classrooms

Melinda J. McBee Orzulak
Bradley University

National Council of Teachers of English
1111 W. Kenyon Road, Urbana, Illinois 61801-1096

Staff Editor: Bonny Graham
Series Editor: Cathy Fleischer
Interior Design: Victoria Pohlmann
Cover Design: Pat Mayer
Cover and Chapter Opening Images: Yasmeen Alzate

NCTE Stock Number: 55646; eStock Number: 55653
ISBN 978-0-8141-5564-6; eISBN 978-0-8141-5565-3

Library of Congress Cataloging-in-Publication Data

Names: McBee Orzulak, Melinda J., 1976- author.
Title: Understanding language : supporting ELL students in responsive ELA classrooms / Melinda J. McBee Orzulak.
Description: Urbana, Illinois : National Council of Teachers of English, 2017 | Series: Principles in practice | Includes bibliographical references and index.
Identifiers: LCCN 2017020877 (print) | LCCN 2017039710 (ebook) | ISBN 9780814155653 | ISBN 9780814155646 (pbk.) | ISBN 9780814155653 (ebook)
Subjects: LCSH: English language—Study and teaching—Foreign speakers. | Education, Bilingual—United States. | Classroom management—United States.
Classification: LCC PE1128.A2 (ebook) | LCC PE1128.A2 M24 2017 (print) | DDC 428.0071—dc23
LC record available at https://lccn.loc.gov/2017020877

For the many teachers and students who play and learn in the ELA sandbox of language every day, especially Maja. And to *mi familia*, especially C and F, that we may play with language for many years to come!

Contents

Acknowledgments

First and foremost, I am deeply grateful to Cathy Fleischer for her feedback on the developing manuscript, as her editorial insights and wordsmithing have truly made this project what it has become. I also thank the other editors, especially Bonny Graham, and reviewers for their thoughtful comments.

I also would like to thank my family for support throughout the writing of this book. It has been such a joy to watch the project grow to fruition along with a first reader who is mostly interested in editing by taking sticky notes off of pages, and who delights me with the daily joys and complications of language acquisition.

Additionally, I offer a special note of thanks to the many teachers and students whose experiences have shaped my thinking and inspired this work. In particular, I offer endless gratitude to Maja, Rachel, Sewak, Ann, Ruth, Meghan, Cole, Eliana, and other teachers who opened up their classrooms and lesson plans to share best practices with me. You inspire me and your students daily! I'm also thankful to the countless teachers (like Ms. Denise of Lingua Garden) who inspire others with their passion for language and positive approach toward students. And I thank Mary Schleppegrell for her generosity with time and resources, along with numerous mentors who have shaped my language understandings, particularly Leslie Rex, Anne Curzan, Donald Freeman, and Anne Ruggles Gere. As my research student, Rachel Shore reviewed and contributed annotated bibliography entries that add to the book's resources, just one more active way she contributes to the field of English teaching. Finally, I thank Bradley University methods students, like Alysen, for inspiring me with ideas for shaping the final text's readability. This work also was supported in part by a Research Excellence Award grant from Bradley University.

Last, this book is seeped in the aromas of thirty-thirty Coffee Co., where the bulk of the manuscript was written and revised in the company of other community members and scholars, particularly my writing partner, Amy. This space reminds me of the importance of safe and welcoming intellectual environments for writing processes—and of all the teachers I've known at countless schools who create those spaces for hundreds of students every year at CICS Northtown Academy, Boston

Arts Academy, Chicago and Peoria Public Schools, and many others from Hawai'i to Illinois to Florida. If I could buy you all a fantastic cup of coffee to express my appreciation and admiration, I would!

NCTE Position Paper on the Role of English Teachers in Educating English Language Learners (ELLs)

Prepared by the NCTE ELL Task Force
Approved by the NCTE Executive Committee, April 2006

This position paper is designed to address the knowledge and skills mainstream teachers need to have in order to develop effective curricula that engage English language learners, develop their academic skills, and help them negotiate their identities as bilingual learners. More specifically, this paper addresses the language and literacy needs of these learners as they participate and learn in English-medium classes. NCTE has made clear bilingual students' right to maintain their native languages (see "On Affirming the CCCC 'Students' Right to Their Own Language'" 2003). Thus, this paper addresses ways teachers can help these students develop English as well as ways they can support their students' bilingualism. In the United States bilingual learners, more commonly referred to as English language learners, are defined as students who know a language other than English and are learning English. Students' abilities range from being non-English speakers to being fully proficient. The recommendations in this paper apply to all of them.

Context

The National Clearinghouse for English Language Acquisition (NCELA) reported that in 2003–04 there were over five million English language learners (ELLs) in schools in the United States (NCELA, 2004). In the last ten years the ELL population has grown 65%, and the diversity of those students continues to challenge teachers and schools. Although 82% of ELLs in the United States are native Spanish speakers, Hopstock and Stephenson (2003) found that school districts identified over 350 different first languages for their second language learners.

Federal, state, and local policies have addressed the education of bilingual learners by implementing different types of programs. Different models of bilingual education, English as a Second Language, English immersion, and integration into mainstream classes, sometimes referred to as submersion, are among the most common approaches. Preferences for the types of programs have changed over time, responding to demographic and political pressures. (For a historical and descriptive summary, see NCTE's "Position Statement on Issues in ESL and Bilingual Education"; Brisk, 2006; Crawford, 2004.)

The best way to educate bilingual learners has been at the center of much controversy. Research points to the advantage of quality bilingual programs (Greene, 1997; Ramirez, 1992; Rolstad, Mahoney, & Glass, 2005; Thomas & Collier, 2002; Willig, 1985) and the benefits of ESL instruction when language is taught through content (Freeman, Y. S., & Freeman, D. E., 1998; Marcia, 2000).

The Role of English Teachers in Educating ELLs

For a variety of reasons, however, the majority of ELLs find themselves in mainstream classrooms taught by teachers with little or no formal professional development in teaching such students (Barron & Menken, 2002; Kindler, 2002). Although improving the education of ELLs has been proposed as a pressing national educational priority (Waxman & Téllez, 2002), many teachers are not adequately prepared to work with a linguistically diverse student population (American Federation of Teachers, 2004; Fillmore & Snow, 2002; Gándara, Rumberger, Maxwell-Jolly, & Callahan, 2003; Menken & Antunez, 2001; Nieto, 2003).

Teachers working to better meet the needs of linguistically diverse students need support. NCTE encourages English teachers to collaborate and work closely with ESL and bilingual teaching professionals, who can offer classroom support, instructional advice, and general insights into second language acquisition. School administrators should support and encourage teachers to attend workshops and professional conferences that regularly offer sessions on bilingual learners, particularly in the areas of reading and writing. Schools should also consider seeking professional development for their teachers from neighboring colleges.

In turn, colleges and universities providing teacher education should offer all preservice teachers, as well as teachers pursuing advanced degree work, preparation in teaching linguistically diverse learners in their future classrooms. Coursework should be offered on second language writing and reading, and on second language acquisition, as well as on culture, and should be encouraged for all teachers.

Who Are the Students?

Bilingual students differ in various ways, including level of oral English proficiency, literacy ability in both the heritage language and English, and cultural backgrounds. English language learners born in the United States often develop conversational language abilities in English but lack academic language proficiency. Newcomers, on the other hand, need to develop both conversational and academic English. Education previous to entering U.S. schools helps determine students' literacy levels in their native language. Some learners may have age-/grade-level skills, while others have limited or no literacy because of the quality of previous schooling, interrupted schooling due to wars or migration, and other circumstances (Suárez-Orozco & Suárez-Orozco, 2001). Given the wide range of English language learners and their backgrounds, it is important that all teachers take the time to learn about their students, particularly in terms of their literacy histories.

Immigrant students and the children of immigrants in the United States come from many cultural backgrounds. The background knowledge English learners bring to school greatly affects their performance. For this reason, teachers of English language learners should be sure to build background for content lessons rather than assuming that bilingual students come with the same background knowledge as mainstream students.

Teaching Bilingual Learners in Mainstream Classrooms

This section specifically addresses teaching language, reading, and writing, as well as the specific kinds of academic literacy that are often a part of most English and language arts

The Role of English Teachers in Educating ELLs

curricula. Although English language arts teachers have literacy as the focus of their teaching, many of these suggestions are useful for teachers working in the content areas as well. To acquire academic content through English, English language learners need to learn English. The academic language that students need in the different content areas differs, and students need scaffolding to help them to learn both the English language and the necessary content. For English language learners, teachers need to consider content objectives as well as English language development objectives.

Bilinguals need three types of knowledge to become literate in a second language. They need to know the second language; they need to know literacy; and they need world knowledge (Bernhardt, 1991). The sections below list key ideas for helping English language learners develop academic English proficiency. More detailed information on the topics covered in this section can be obtained from the topical bibliography compiled as part of this project.

To teach bilingual learners, teachers must get to know their learners.

Knowledge of the Students

Knowledge of the students is key to good teaching. Because teachers relate to students both as learners and as children or adolescents, teachers must establish how they will address these two types of relationships, what they need to know about their students, and how they will acquire this knowledge. The teacher-learner relationship implies involvement between teachers and students around subject matter and language and literacy proficiency in both languages. Adult-child relationships are more personal and should include the family. Focusing on both types of relationships bridges the gap between school and the world outside it, a gap that is especially important for many bilingual students whose world differs greatly from school.

Teaching Language

Second language learners need to develop academic proficiency in English to master content-area subjects. Teachers can provide effective instruction for these students by:

- Recognizing that second language acquisition is a gradual developmental process and is built on students' knowledge and skill in their native language;
- Providing authentic opportunities to use language in a nonthreatening environment;
- Teaching key vocabulary connected with the topic of the lesson;
- Teaching academic oral language in the context of various content areas;
- Teaching text- and sentence-level grammar in context to help students understand the structure and style of the English language;
- Teaching the specific features of language students need to communicate in social as well as academic contexts.

The Role of English Teachers in Educating ELLs

Teaching Literacy: Reading

Bilingual students also need to learn to read and write effectively in order to succeed in school.

Teachers can support English language learners' literacy development by:

- Introducing classroom reading materials that are culturally relevant;
- Connecting the readings with the students' background knowledge and experiences;
- Encouraging students to discuss the readings, including the cultural dimensions of the text;
- Having students read a more accessible text on the topic before reading the assigned text;
- Asking families to read with students a version in the heritage language;
- Replacing discrete skill exercises and drills with many opportunities to read;
- Providing opportunities for silent reading in either the students' first language or in English;
- Reading aloud frequently to allow students to become familiar with and appreciate the sounds and structures of written language;
- Reading aloud while students have access to the text to facilitate connecting oral and written modalities;
- Stimulating students' content knowledge of the text before introducing the text;
- Teaching language features, such as text structure, vocabulary, and text- and sentence-level grammar to facilitate comprehension of the text;
- Recognizing that first and second language growth increases with abundant reading and writing.

Support reading comprehension by:

- Relating the topic to the cultural experiences of the students;
- "Front loading" comprehension via a walk through the text or a preview of the main ideas, and other strategies that prepare students for the topic of the text;
- Having students read a more accessible text on the topic before reading the assigned text;
- Asking families to read with students a version in the heritage language;
- Doing pre-reading activities that elicit discussion of the topic;
- Teaching key vocabulary essential for the topic;
- Recognizing that experiences in writing can be used to clarify understanding of reading.

Teaching Literacy: Writing

Writing well in English is often the most difficult skill for English language learners to master. Many English language learners are still acquiring vocabulary and syntactic competence in their writing. Students may show varying degrees of acquisition, and not all second language writers will have the same difficulties or challenges. Teachers should be aware that English language learners may not be familiar with terminology and routines often associated with writing instruction in the United States, including writing process, drafting, revision, editing, workshop, conference, audience, purpose, or genre. Furthermore, certain elements of discourse, particularly in terms of audience and persuasion, may differ across cultural contexts. The same is true for textual borrowing and plagiarism. The CCCC Statement on Second Language Writing and Writers is a useful resource for all teachers of writing to examine.

Teachers can provide instructional support for English language learners in their writing by:

- Providing a nurturing environment for writing;
- Introducing cooperative, collaborative writing activities which promote discussion;
- Encouraging contributions from all students, and promoting peer interaction to support learning;
- Replacing drills and single-response exercises with time for writing practice;
- Providing frequent meaningful opportunities for students to generate their own texts;
- Designing writing assignments for a variety of audiences, purposes, and genres, and scaffolding the writing instruction;
- Providing models of well-organized papers for the class. Teachers should consider glossing sample papers with comments that point to the specific aspects of the paper that make it well written;
- Offering comments on the strength of the paper, in order to indicate areas where the student is meeting expectations;
- Making comments explicit and clear (both in written response and in oral responses). Teachers should consider beginning feedback with global comments (content and ideas, organization, thesis) and then move on to more local concerns (or mechanical errors) when student writers are more confident with the content of their draft;
- Giving more than one suggestion for change—so that students still maintain control of their writing;
- Not assuming that every learner understands how to cite sources or what plagiarism is. Teachers should consider talking openly about citation and plagiarism in class, exploring the cultural values that are implicit in the rules of plagiarism and textual borrowing, and noting that not all cultures ascribe to the same rules and guidelines. Students should be provided with strategies for avoiding plagiarism.

Teaching Language and Content

The best way to help students learn both English and the knowledge of school subjects is to teach language through content. This should not replace reading and writing instruction in English, nor study of literature and grammar. There are three key reasons to do this:

1. **Students get both language and content.**
   Research has shown that students can learn English and subject matter content material

at the same time. Students don't need to delay the study of science or literature until they reach high levels of English. Instead, they can learn both simultaneously. Given the time limitations older students face, it is crucial that classes provide them with both academic content-area knowledge and academic English.

2. **Language is kept in its natural context.**
When teachers teach science in English, students learn science terms as they study biology or chemistry. The vocabulary occurs naturally as students read and discuss science texts.
3. **Students have reasons to use language for real purposes.**
The primary purpose of school is to help students develop the knowledge of different academic disciplines. When academic content is presented in English, students focus on the main purpose of schooling: learning science, math, social studies, or literature. In the process, they also learn English.

Selecting Materials

- Choose a variety of texts around a theme.
- Choose texts at different levels of difficulty.
- Choose reading and writing materials that represent the cultures of the students in the class.
- When possible, include texts in the native languages of the ELLs in the class. The following considerations should be used as a guide for choosing texts that support bilingual learners:
  - Materials should include both literature and informational texts.
  - Materials should include culturally relevant texts.
  - Authentic materials should be written to inform or entertain, not to teach a grammar point or a letter-sound correspondence.
  - The language of the text should be natural.
  - If translated, the translation should be good language.
  - Materials should include predictable text for emergent readers.
  - Materials should include texts with nonlinguistic cues that support comprehension. (For a more comprehensive checklist, see Freeman, Y. S., & Freeman, D. E., 2002; Freeman, D. E., & Freeman, Y. S., 2004.)

Low-Level Literacy Immigrant Students

Late-arrival immigrant and refugee students with low literacy skills have been found to benefit from Newcomer programs or Welcome Centers designed for 1–3 semesters of high school (Boyson & Short, 2003; Schnur, 1999; Short, 2002). The focus is to help students acquire beginning English skills and guide students' acculturation to the U.S. school system before enrollment in regular ESL language support programs or content-area classrooms. The integration of such programs in high school English departments should be encouraged.

The Role of English Teachers in Educating ELLs

Conclusion

As the number of bilingual learners in mainstream classes increases, it becomes even more important for mainstream teachers to use effective practices to engage these students so that they can acquire the academic English and the content-area knowledge they need for school success. The guidelines offered here are designed as initial suggestions for teachers to follow. However, we recognize that all teachers need much more. Teachers need continued support and professional development to enable all their students, including their bilingual students, to succeed.

References

American Federation of Teachers. (March, 2004). *Closing the achievement gap: Focus on Latino students* (Policy Brief 17). Retrieved March 28, 2006, from http://www.aft.org/teachers/pusbs-reports/index.htm#english.

Barron, V., & Menken, K. (2002). *What are the characteristics of the bilingual education and ESL teacher shortage?* Washington, D.C.: National Clearinghouse for English Language Acquisition and Language Instruction Educational Programs.

Bernhardt, E. B. (1991). A psycholinguistic perspective on second language literacy. Reading in Two Languages. *AILA Review*, *8*, 31–44.

Boyson, B. A., & Short, D. J. (2003). *Secondary school newcomer programs in the United States* (Research Report 12). Santa Cruz, CA, and Washington, DC: Center for Research on Education Diversity & Excellence.

Brisk, M. E. (2006). *Bilingual education: From compensatory to quality schooling*. (2nd ed.) Mahwah, NJ: Erlbaum.

Crawford, J. (2004). *Educating English learners*. Los Angeles: Bilingual Education Services.

De Jong, E. J. (2002). Effective bilingual education: From theory to academic achievement in a two-way bilingual program. *Bilingual Research Journal*, *26*(1), 1–15.

Fillmore, L. W., & Snow, C. (2002). What teachers need to know about language. In C. T. Adger, C. Snow, & D. Christian (Eds.), *What teachers need to know about language* (pp. 7–53). Washington, DC: Center for Applied Linguistics.

Freeman, D. E., and Freeman, Y. S. (2004). *Essential linguistics: What you need to know to teach reading, ESL, spelling, phonics, and grammar*. Portsmouth, NH: Heinemann.

Freeman, Y. S., & Freeman, D. E. (1998). *ESL/EFL teaching: Principles for success*. Portsmouth, NH: Heinemann.

Freeman, Y. S., and Freeman, D. E. (2002). *Closing the achievement gap*. Portsmouth, NH: Heinemann.

Gándara, P., Rumberger, R., Maxwell-Jolly, J., & Callahan, R. (2003). English learners in California schools: Unequal resources, unequal outcomes. *Education Policy Analysis Archives*, *11*(36). Retrieved March 28, 2006, from http://epaa.asu.edu/.

Gibbons, P. (2002). *Scaffolding language, scaffolding learning: Teaching second language learners in the mainstream classroom*. Portsmouth, NH: Heinemann.

Greene, J. P. (1997). A meta-analysis of the Rossell and Baker review of bilingual education research. *Bilingual Research Journal*, *21*.

The Role of English Teachers in Educating ELLs

Hopstock, P. & Stephenson, T. (2003). *Native languages of limited English proficient students.* U.S. Department of Education. Retrieved March 5, 2006.

Kindler, A. L. (2002). *Survey of the states' limited English proficient students and available educational programs and services 1999–2000 summary report.* Washington, DC: National Clearinghouse for English Language Acquisition and Language Instruction Education Programs (NCELA). Retrieved Dec. 26, 2003, from http://www.ncela.gwu.edu.

Krashen, S. (1996). *Under attack: The case against bilingual education.* Culver City, CA: Language Education Associates.

McQuillan, J., & Tse, L. (1997). Does research matter? An analysis of media opinion of bilingual education, 1984–1994. *Bilingual Research Journal, 20*(1), 1–27.

Menken, K., & Antunez, B. (2001). *An overview of the preparation and certification of teachers working with limited English proficient students.* Washington, DC: National Clearinghouse of Bilingual Education. Retrieved July 28, 2003, from http://www.ericsp.org/pages/digests/ncbe.pdf.

NCELA. (2006). *The growing number of limited English proficient students 1991–2002.* Washington, DC: U.S. Department of Education.

Nieto, S. M. (2003). *What keeps teachers going?* New York: Teachers College.

Pally, M. (Ed.) (2000). *Sustained content teaching in academic ESL/EFL: A practical approach.* Boston: Houghton Mifflin.

Ramirez, J. D. (1992). Executive summary. *Bilingual Research Journal, 16,* 1–62.

Rolstad, K., Mahoney, K., & Glass, G. V. (2005). The big picture: A meta-analysis of program effectiveness research on English language learners. *Educational Policy, 19,* 572–594.

Schnur, B. (1999). A newcomer's high school. *Educational Leadership, 56*(7), 50–52.

Short, D. J. (2002). Newcomer programs: An educational alternative for secondary immigrant students. *Education and Urban Society 34*(2), 173–198.

Solomon, J., & Rhodes, N. (1995). *Conceptualizing academic language.* Washington, DC: The National Center for Research on Cultural Diversity and Second Language Learning.

Suárez-Orozco, C., & Suárez-Orozco, M. M. (2001). *Children of immigration.* Cambridge, MA: Harvard University.

Thomas, W. P., & Collier, V. P. (2002). *A national study of school effectiveness for language minority students' long-term academic achievement.* Santa Cruz, CA: Center for Research on Education, Diversity & Excellence, University of California, Santa Cruz.

Waxman, H. C., & Téllez, K. (2002). *Research synthesis on effective teaching practices for English language learners* (Publication Series No. 3). Philadelphia: Mid-Atlantic Regional Educational Laboratory.

Willig, A. C. (1985). A meta-analysis of selected studies on the effectiveness of bilingual education. *Review of Educational Research, 55*(3), 269–317.

For more resources to support English language learners, see http://www.ncte.org/positions/statements/teacherseducatingell.

Statement of Terminology and Glossary

Steven Alvarez, St. John's University
Betsy Gilliland, University of Hawai'i Mānoa
Christina Ortmeier-Hooper, University of New Hampshire
Melinda J. McBee Orzulak, Bradley University
Shannon Pella, California State University, Sacramento

As authors of the various books in the Teaching English Language Learners strand of the NCTE Principles in Practice (PIP) imprint, we have made a concerted effort to use consistent terminology in these volumes. All of us have thought long and hard about the ways in which we label and describe bilingual and ELL students and the programs that often provide these students with additional support. Even so, readers will notice some variation in terms used to describe students, classrooms, and teaching practices. The concern over terminology is part of a long-standing discussion and trends in the labeling of these students, as well as of the fields that conduct research on teachers and students working across languages to teach and learn English. Often the shifting among terms leads to confusion and contention for teachers, administrators, teacher educators, and policymakers.

To address this confusion and tension, we begin each book in this strand with a glossary of common terms and acronyms that are part of current discussions about meeting the needs of these students in English language arts classrooms and beyond. For many readers, the terms themselves and the ongoing shift to new terms can be alienating, the jargon dividing readers into insiders and outsiders. But often the shift in terms has a great deal to do with both policy and issues of identity for students. For example, up until the No Child Left Behind (NCLB) Act of 2001, most educational documents referred to these students as *bilingual* or *ESL*, both of which acknowledge that English is a second language and that a student has a first language as well.

The term *English language learner* was adopted with NCLB and brought into our schools and the larger public discourse. In fact, in 2002 the US Department of Education renamed the Office of Bilingual Education and Minority Languages Affairs. It became the Office of English Language Acquisition, Language Enhancement and Academic Achievement for Limited English Proficient Students, now identified simply as the Office of English Language Acquisition (OELA). The change indicated a shift away from acknowledging students' home languages or bilingual abilities. Close to two decades later, the term *English language learner* remains prominent in educational policy and in many textbooks geared toward teachers and teacher educators. Its prominence and familiarity in the literature makes it an accessible way to talk about these students. Yet, as we have heard from many students through the years, the term *English language learner* can also be limiting. As one student asked, "When do I stop being an English language learner and get to just be an English language user?" The term also works against efforts to acknowledge the competencies and linguistically sophisticated talents these students have as translators, bilingual speakers, and cross-cultural negotiators.

Statement of Terminology and Glossary

In these PIP volumes, we use the term *English language learner* as a way to reach out to readers who see and hear this term regularly used in their schools, in their hallways, and in other helpful books in the field. However, some of us also use the terms *multilingual* or *bilingual* in order to encourage a discussion of these young people not simply as novice English learners but as individuals with linguistic and academic competencies they have gained from bilingual/multilingual experiences and literacies.

Glossary

Bilingual, multilingual, or plurilingual: These terms refer to the ability to use (i.e., speak, write, and/or read) multiple languages. For many ELL-designated students in US schools, English is actually the third or fourth language they have learned, making *bilingual* not necessarily an accurate term.

Emergent bilingual: This term has been proposed as a more appropriate term than *LEP* or *ELL*, because it points to possibilities of developing bilingualism rather than focusing on language limits or deficiencies (García, 2009).

English as a foreign language (EFL): Refers to non-native English-speaking students who are learning English in a country where English is not the primary language.

English as an international language (EIL) or English as a lingua franca (ELF): These are terms used to refer to global conceptions of English, or English used for communication between members of various nations.

English as a second language (ESL): Readers may be most familiar with this term because it has been used as an overarching term for students, programs, and/or a field of study. Currently the term usually refers to programs of instruction (i.e., study of English in an English-speaking country); however, *ESL* was used in the past to refer to English language learning students.

English language learner (ELL): In keeping with the terminology used in the *NCTE Position Paper on the Role of English Teachers in Educating English Language Learners (ELLs)*, this PIP strand employs the term *ELL*, which is commonly used in secondary schools as the short form of *English language learner*. The term refers to a complex, heterogeneous range of students who are in the process of learning English.

English learner (EL): This is the preferred term of the California Department of Education (and, increasingly, other states). California is the state with the largest number and percentage of emergent bilingual students enrolled in public schools. Over the past twenty years, California has moved from *LEP* to *ELL* and, most recently, from *ELL* to *EL*.

First language (L1) and second language (L2): *L1* has been used to refer to students' "mother tongue" or "home language" as they learn additional languages (referred to as *L2*).

Generation 1.5: This term, originally used in higher education, often refers to students who have been long-term residents in the United States but who were born abroad (al-

Statement of Terminology and Glossary

though the term is sometimes also used to refer to US-born children of recent immigrants). The designation of 1.5 describes their feelings of being culturally between first- and second-generation immigrants; they are often fluent in spoken English but may still be working to command aspects of written English, especially academic writing. As long-term residents, these students may reject *ESL* as a term that has been used to refer to recent immigrants to the United States.

Limited English proficiency (LEP): This abbreviation may be used in some educational contexts to refer to a designation used by the US Department of Education. Many scholars see this as a deficit term because of its focus on subtractive language (language that implies a deficiency) under a monolingual assumption of proficiency.

Long-term English language learner (LTELL): Currently in use in some states, this term refers to K–12 students who have been enrolled in US schools for many years and continue to be stuck with the ELL designation long past the time it should take for redesignation. Like Generation 1.5 students, LTELLs may have spent most if not all of their education in US schools. For a variety of reasons, including family mobility, inconsistent educational programs, and personal reasons, they have not had opportunities to learn academic language sufficiently to pass English language proficiency tests and other measures of proficiency for redesignation (Olsen, 2010).

Mainstream: This term is increasingly antiquated due to shifting demographics in the United States. In practice, it often refers to nonremedial, nonhonors, nonsheltered classes and programs. Sometimes it is used to refer to native or monolingual English speakers as a norm; changing demographics, however, mean that schools increasingly have a majority of culturally and linguistically diverse students, so it's been argued that a linguistically diverse classroom is the "New Mainstream" (Enright, 2011).

Monolingual: This term is used to refer to people who speak only one language, although often this label masks speakers' fluent use of multiple dialects, or variations, of English—an issue of particular concern when working with culturally diverse students who use other varieties of English (such as Hawai'i Pidgin or African American Vernacular) in their lives outside of school. The monolingual English label can mask these diverse students' need to learn academic English just as much as their immigrant classmates do. Much of what this PIP strand discusses is relevant to students who utilize multiple varieties of English; teachers can support these students by acknowledging their multilingualism and helping them learn to use English for academic and other purposes.

Native or non-native English speakers (NES, NNES): Some materials contrast native English speakers (NES) with non-native English speakers (NNES). As with *monolingual*, the term *native speaker* is increasingly unclear, given how many long-term ELLs speak English fluently without a "foreign" accent and yet technically have another world language as their home or first language.

Newcomer: Some school districts have separate one-year programs for "newcomers," or students who are newly arrived in the United States, in which students learn not just "surviv-

Statement of Terminology and Glossary

al" English, but also how school works in the United States. As the position statement discusses, it's sometimes argued that newcomer programs benefit "low-level literacy immigrant students" and/or students with interrupted formal education who may have limited literacy in their first language (L1). Other newcomers may be fully literate in L1, especially by high school, and may or may not benefit from being isolated from the mainstream curriculum. For older students, the challenge is to move away from "low-level" ideas of literacy assessment that may discount the literacies of these students.

Resident or local bilingual, multilingual, or plurilingual: These terms are sometimes used to refer to students who reside in the United States (in contrast to those who are on student visas). Resident students may or may not be US citizens, others may not have permanent resident status, while still others may not have immigration documentation at all.

References

Enright, K. A. (2011). Language and literacy for a new mainstream. *American Educational Research Journal, 48*(1), 80–118. doi: 10.3102/0002831210368989

García, O. (2009). Emergent bilinguals and TESOL: What's in a name? *TESOL Quarterly, 43*(2), 322–26. doi:10.1002/j.1545-7249.2009.tb00172.x

Olsen, L. (2010). *Reparable harm: Fulfilling the unkept promise of educational opportunity for California's long term English learners*. Long Beach, CA: Californians Together.

Introducing the Principles

Recognizing Strengths

Chapter One

My Journey to Understanding ELL Students in the ELA Classroom

The Realization of What I Didn't Know

In one of my earliest secondary school teaching experiences as a full-time teaching volunteer in a school for long-term suspended students, I visited the family of one of my students, Arturo.[1] As I stood in the living room among the carefully arranged family pictures and the Spanish-language Bible on the shelf, Arturo began speaking rapid-fire Spanish with his mother. Struggling to follow along with my limited high school Spanish, I had new insight into my student: suddenly, I was privy to a whole set of his language skills that had been invisible to me up to that point, especially his oral language fluency in this different context and his level of literacy in a language other than English. Over time and continued teaching, I began to appreciate how students like Arturo are able to communicate in different languages or varieties of English with different audiences, an appreciation that became a key to a new understanding of language.

1. Pseudonyms are used throughout this book for names of students, teachers, and schools unless a teacher has specified otherwise.

As my teaching career continued, I began to take note of the specific ways many students (not just English language learners) struggled to understand Shakespearean English as we read *Hamlet* and of the writing patterns for students who spoke American Sign Language or who had recently moved to Boston from Haiti. These experiences helped me notice the many facets of language (oral, written, academic, and social) and the complex ways that language played out in the English language arts (ELA) classroom. I noticed how issues of multiple English language varieties, as well as multilingual language learning, challenged the beliefs I (and many other teachers, I believe) held about what it meant to be a "good" English teacher. Most prominent of these is the belief that we are the keepers of a singular English that's valued in all contexts and with all audiences. This belief, I learned, can obscure the ways that better understanding of the complexity of language can help us as ELA teachers be more responsive to students, especially linguistically and culturally diverse students.

My point is that as we consider language understandings in our teaching of English language learners (ELLs) and others, we must consider *What counts as language?* and *What do we mean by "language"?* Do we mean, as the Common Core State Standards (CCSS) suggest, that language means conventions, vocabulary acquisition, and/or "grammar"? Or is it something more? When I first started teaching, I mostly thought in the CCSS way: seeing language as a tool that helped us to communicate. Years later, I learned new ways of thinking about language from researchers and linguists in a second language interest group at the University of Michigan: seeing language as an emergent, dynamic system (Ellis & Larsen-Freeman, 2006) and learning about the inextricable links between language, concepts, and culture.

Several years after my experience with Arturo, teaching at a school in Chicago where my students came from a wide range of backgrounds, I began to expand my understanding of language in connection to bilingualism—or multilingualism, to be more accurate. I realized that while many of my students spoke English with the same accent I did, the grammatical patterns that emerged in their writing surprised me. I wondered if these students were bilingual even though they didn't seem to be what I thought of as English as a second language (ESL) students. Surprisingly, some of these students struggled in their Spanish classes, unable to take the second-level Spanish class at our school, even though their parents spoke Spanish at home. As I watched these multilingual students try to figure out which language class to take, I realized that I couldn't make assumptions about links between culture and language ability.

Increasingly, I began to recognize the importance of language variation for all speakers of English. While I am aware that teaching about language variation as a second language can be problematic politically (e.g., the Oakland Controversy, or "Ebonics Debate"), I came to learn that language variety can be a reality for all students, including for ELLs or multilingual students who may also learn different language varieties, such as what has been described as "Spanglish" or Chicano English. The reality is that a wide range of students, not just ELLs, experience academic language struggles. Recent calls to look at students' *code-meshing* (the merging of different language varieties, or codes) remind us that in today's increasingly global and wired communities, it is important to support all of our students' needs for linguistic flexibility in English—academic, social, and meshed versions of academic and social English. Further, we as teachers must understand the realities of language learning that takes place prior to and outside of schooling. We need to gauge the linguistic depth students already have, whether these linguistic elements are due to English language variation or to second, third, and fourth languages. In sum, we need to be able to apply a sociolinguistic perspective of patterns available to students rather than fixating on "errors." This sociolinguistic perspective means that we explore the varied ways language use interrelates with power dynamics, identities, cultures, and contexts.

Over time, it also dawned on me how many benefits my multilingual students brought to our engagement with ELA content. I saw that many of my assumptions about what counts as "language" and which students in my classrooms brought varied language use were dead wrong, and I wondered about the ways complicated *language beliefs* intersected with *language use*. I had assumed that multilingual students would value their home languages. In reality, though, I found that not all students valued their ability to use multiple languages, and some teachers saw multilingual students as simply posing problems, not adding rich resources to their classes. Some ELL students took the fervent position that English should be the only language used in the United States. Yet these same students enjoyed writing poems that incorporated Spanish and English or Polish and English, translated for their families during family conferences, or went to Ukrainian language school on Saturdays.

I also realized that one of my (erroneous) underlying language understandings was that language use was easy to identify and that it would be obvious to me if students knew other languages. Without familiarity with second language acquisition, I was like many teachers who interpret some students as more "fluent" than others because of their oral language skills and didn't always notice the support students needed for academic language. I began to realize how much simpler it was to step into the traditional ELA teacher role in language study—e.g., to drill on format and grammar based on assumptions about the transfer of grammar or vocabulary exercises to actual writing. Many of my ELL students actually liked these cut-and-dried grammar lessons. Unfortunately, the transfer to their writing was often minimal at best.

I felt overwhelmed by what I didn't know about my students and their language use, even as I worked with limited support staff providing English language support, special education support, and translation for families. I was unsure about so many things: Should I call students' homes without a translator? How could I (or even should I) help a student edit a poem written in her home language? Should I ask for help from my Spanish teacher colleague? What should I do with my students who regularly spoke Russian, French, or other languages when all I knew was English and a little Spanish?

My "aha" moment from all this observation and wondering came down to this: language in all its variation and difference is complex. It's not enough to just "appreciate" multilingual students' language abilities in some kind of abstract manner. We have to understand facets of language use and acquisition to really understand and use students' assets in ELA teaching. We also have to understand myths about language and multilingualism that can obscure our deployment of best practice. These understandings (and misunderstandings) about language can be overwhelming as a teacher.

Scholars have described a long list of potential myths, such as that learning two languages confuses people, that there is one stable English used in all contexts, that correcting errors should always happen right away, that speaking a language well means someone is fluent, or that recent immigrants are the first immigrants to ever want bilingual education or to refuse to learn English—all of these myths and others are still in circulation. (See Soltero [2011] for a full discussion of conscious and unconscious myths related to language.) We need to consider this complicated landscape of language and not be intimidated by what we don't know. The questions we ask help us better understand the many assets of our multilingual students, —as well as the assets they (and our more complex understandings of language) can bring to our classrooms.

The Quest to Learn More

Determined to learn more about the patterns that seemed to be emerging in some of my writers' prose, I took a summer course to extend my Spanish language knowledge. This course opened my eyes to the language variations that exist not only in Spanish but also in the many other languages that were part of my students' lives. I began to notice the ways verbs, like the subjunctive, functioned; the ways differences in word order (like more flexibility in word order in Spanish) influenced students' syntax; how long noun groups used in academic language could be challenging when the first language usually places modifiers after nouns; the ways alphabet differences could cause challenges (as in Arabic); the ways differences in levels of language modality affected understanding; how articles might or might not be used (as in Russian). I applied some of my new knowledge in my teaching, and then continued to learn by attending professional development sessions focused on the challenges of teaching English language learners with a variety of first languages and on ways of supporting reading and writing in diverse schools. I attended sessions at the National Council of Teachers of English (NCTE) Annual Convention and learned from other teachers. Later, as I learned more about educational linguistics and read about second language acquisition and approaches to teaching English language learners, I began to understand some of the complexities inherent in my experiences.

I started to realize over time that a simple understanding of English as a second language is not enough to support the range of learners who are the new reality in the "mainstream" classroom. As I taught, I began to realize:

- I couldn't always tell which students were multilingual based on accents.
- Some students who were multilingual already interpreted their abilities as deficits, so they wouldn't admit to outside language use.
- Some patterns would emerge based on home language use, but not always.
- Some of my best, worst, and average writers and readers fit the category of "ELL" or multilingual learner.
- Rigid grammar book instruction helped none of us.

Over time, as I began to complicate my understanding of multilingual students, I started to notice something else: the many joys of having a multilingual ELA classroom, in particular that students who had multiple language abilities could offer a lot to our discussions of language, grammar, and much more. Initially, I was distracted from seeing this benefit because I was so focused on my need for resources. A deeper understanding of the demands of language learning (written, oral, academic, and other), as well as of culture and language and many other areas, was a benefit to be mined in my classroom.

The Discovery of Possibilities from Understanding Language: Benefits for All

What does it mean to understand language? You may be like me and need resources to fully experience the joys of understanding how language is used in multiple and exciting ways in your classroom. You may have some of the same issues I did, like the need to better understand the complexities surrounding ELL students in a mainstream classroom. You may need more information about what the range of "language learners" looks like. You may need clarification about why some strategies are working and/or not working. You may just need some new ideas. You may be encountering linguistic diversity for the first time, in a new context, or with a new group of students. You may have a recent addition to your classroom who has changed the teaching and learning dynamic. You may be noticing variations in your students' writing and reading approaches, strengths, and skills but aren't sure what to do next. Or you may be a new or preservice teacher who is aware of your limited preparation for teaching ELLs or who wants to extend your initial insights.

You are not alone. I'm painfully aware that my limited knowledge of ELL students stymied my own instruction at times, similar to the way I now see many new teachers approaching their ELLs. In my current research in my role as an English educator, I've learned that new teachers often experience surprises based on language and/or the complexity of linguistic diversity in their classrooms. Inevitably, dynamics of language and power emerge in classroom interactions. One unfortunate reaction I've noted is that many mainstream teachers see ELL students either as the purview of someone else or as a problem to be overcome.

My journey shows me something different: that ELL students *should* be our purview because understanding language is key to improving ELA instruction for all students. Our mainstream ELA classrooms provide crucial opportunities for academic and interpersonal language learning, and these opportunities are even richer in a multilingual classroom.

I've titled this book *Understanding Language*, intentionally using the *–ing* verb tense, or progressive tense, to show that learning to understand language remains an ongoing process due to the varied contexts, time periods, and interactions in which we live, learn, and teach. That's one reason why in each chapter I ask you to consider questions to get you started on new steps in the process. And because language is intensely personal and individual as well as embedded in much larger cultural, institutional, and interpersonal contexts, I've framed each chapter with my own experiences as well as those of other teachers, some of whom are multilingual themselves and others who are functionally monolingual like me. Understanding language means considering how our own experiences, and those of our students, intersect with myths about language, as well as with the oral, written, academic, and social uses of language. Better understanding language allows us to shift from deficit-based to asset-based understandings.

Challenge or Opportunity? Language Choices for Framing and Perceiving Reality

As an illustration of how metaphors and beliefs shape understandings of teaching English language learners, consider the following terms often used to describe language use and ELL students:

- Bi-/multilingual
- Challenge
- Contributors
- Double the work
- Fluent
- Strength
- Home language
- Learner
- Limited
- Monolingual
- Potential
- Problem
- Proficient
- Second language
- Surprise

Which terms do you see as positive, negative, or neutral?

Look at Figure 1.1. Is this how you classified the terms? Are there other terms you might add?

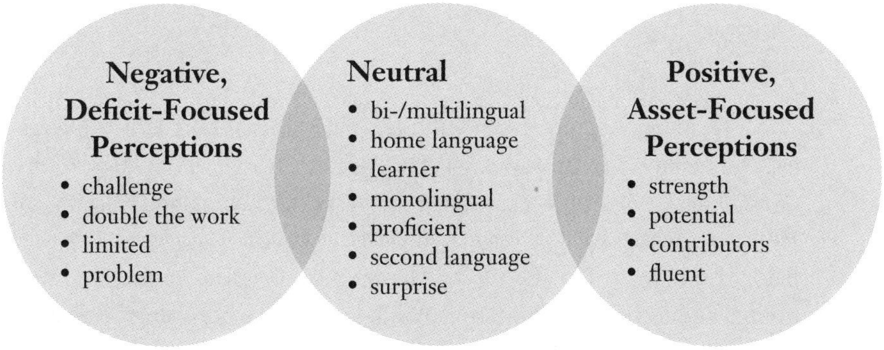

Negative, Deficit-Focused Perceptions
- challenge
- double the work
- limited
- problem

Neutral
- bi-/multilingual
- home language
- learner
- monolingual
- proficient
- second language
- surprise

Positive, Asset-Focused Perceptions
- strength
- potential
- contributors
- fluent

Figure 1.1. Perceptions of ELL students and language understandings.

Keep these terms in mind as you continue reading as I suggest why and how metaphors matter.

Why Our Metaphors Matter

> I realized that having ELL students is like having a gift.
> —Sewak, early-career English teacher

> They're our bread and butter.
> —Maja, experienced English teacher

In this book, I'll be drawing on key principles and teachers' examples to help us shift from deficit-focused ways of understanding linguistically diverse students and their language in our classrooms toward asset-focused ways. By showing how principles can play out in practice, this book can help teachers recognize and apply the ways teaching ELL students draws on and strengthens best practice in ELA instruction.

Metaphors are an important way we frame the world around us—and for teachers, this framing can impact not only our relationships with students but also their success in our classrooms. For instance, in some multicultural classrooms, the metaphor of teacher as helper has been shown to be less effective than the metaphor of teacher as intercultural communicator (Hyland, 2005). *Helper* in this case implies a more patronizing model, whereas *intercultural communicator* implies a sense of two-way exchange that recognizes the need for mutual learning and appreciation.

Seeing ourselves as *intercultural communicators* creates opportunities for two-way exchange that recognizes the need for mutual learning and appreciation.

Thinking metaphorically can help us understand the ELL students in our classrooms in different ways: as a challenge or surprise, as an opportunity or asset, or as someone else's problem. Over my years of teaching and learning, these different metaphors have all resonated with me at various points as I've shifted from being overwhelmed by the gaping chasm in my language understandings to being excited about the possibilities for building bridges, or creating intricate gridwork, as I learn more about language while I teach and learn with students. Paying attention to these metaphors is important because they shape how we understand language in the spaces of our classrooms. When ELL students are framed as a challenge, a difficulty, or something external to our "regular classrooms," we cast them as burdens or interlopers. What happens if instead we frame these students—and especially our need to understand how they do use and can use language—as an opportunity? While we still may feel "under water" or overloaded at times, how might this reframing help us as teachers?

Understanding the strengths brought to ELA instruction by ELL students is something I wish I had recognized earlier in my teaching. I wish I'd known more about so many areas of how language works, such as distinctions between oral and written language practices, which would have helped me create a richer language learning environment for all students.

This book is a response to what I wish I had known as a classroom teacher, especially in my early years of teaching language learners of various types. It focuses on research and teaching examples that provide glimpses into experienced classroom teaching that honors the strengths available in linguistically diverse classes.

In Practice: The Strengths ELL Students Bring to ELA Classrooms and Our Understandings as Intercultural Communicators

Key Practices in This Vignette

- Incorporating and valuing students' perspectives and experiences
- Building on students' assets (visual literacies and cultural experiences)
- Understanding opportunities that exist in multilingual classrooms
- Seeing oneself as an intercultural communicator
- Considering varieties of English—regional, international, academic

Florida teacher Sewak, who grew up in Chicago with strong roots in the Caribbean, describes how the strengths of ELL students add to the "taste and flavor of the class. It can give you prompts for discussion and it gives you a larger variety [of perspectives and experiences]." Sewak was sensitized to the struggles of ELL students from a young age, as he saw how his cousins who used Caribbean English initially struggled with their schoolwork because they didn't always use the same sentence structure and lexicon as other English-speaking students. Further, his own multilingualism shapes his appreciation for how language affects our classrooms and helps him see languages as an asset in ELA learning.

For instance, students can discuss the cultural backgrounds that influence their interpretation of literature. They can unpack the way their visual literacy (i.e., how they interpret images) can be influenced by where they grew up, their cultural references and texts, and/or artwork in their home communities. Sewak's ninth-grade ELA classes include ELL students from varied backgrounds—many who are newcomers to the United States and placed directly in his class—and he uses the first week of school to lay the groundwork for a welcoming and engaged learning community.

To do so, Sewak assigns an About Me paper as an opening activity to start establishing students' comfort level in the classroom and to emphasize the importance of cultural and family background to their class learning as a team. In the paper, students respond to multiple questions asking them to describe their families, cultures, and backgrounds using both words and images (pictures or drawings).

Sewak models by sharing his own About Me example that includes both words and images, purposely highlighting a picture answer first to show the value of using an image and to encourage students to use their own images; the goal is to build comfort levels for newcomer ELL students who may be able to express more with image-based answers at this point in their language learning.

Sewak points to a picture of brightly lit lamps on his paper: "Here's an example of culture, a cultural festival. You may not know that in my family's Caribbean background, Diwali is celebrated, a Festival of Lights. This lamp represents that festival so important to my cultural background." Further explaining the importance of their culture

continued on next page

to his family, Sewak points to a coconut and describes the huge role of coconuts in various everyday and special occasion foods he grew up eating, explaining the role of coconuts as a major export in the region of his family's origin.

After Sewak shares his examples, students begin making connections, saying, "Wait, I have something like that in my culture, too." They add pictures to their own About Me papers, which they share with the group while sitting in one large circle, a structure Sewak uses to help students take immediate ownership as part of the class. The group considers, "What is my culture?" And students who never thought of a particular holiday or tradition as culture begin noticing comparisons and clarifying how events or experiences reflect important aspects of their familial and cultural backgrounds.

This emphasis on cross-cultural and community-based learning continues throughout the year in Sewak's class. On Fridays, during the last ten minutes of class, two students share a picture that represents a recent event, world connection, or family tradition that is important to them. Eventually, a giant bulletin board labeled "Who We Are" includes images from the 150 students in Sewak's classes.

This awareness of identities, cultures, and values becomes a key part of the students' ongoing engagement with ELA texts. Before each new text they read, students turn to a Reflection section in their binders and write predictions and connections based on an initial overview of the text. In these reflections, students frequently draw on events, experiences, and cultural traditions they have shared in class, making connections between literary characters, themes, settings, and their own lives.

For example, this sense of familiarity and ownership enriches their group reading of a story about a family broken down by war in the Middle East. At first many students see the story as disconnected from their lives, until one student (from a different war-torn country) describes firsthand personal experiences as a teenager leaving home during war and even shares images, helping the group make connections to the short story. When reading *The Odyssey*, students consider how cultures and traditions interrelate with the story (and their own experiences), eventually combining a Socratic seminar with a food festival.

Sewak's goal is for students to learn about themselves and one another—noticing commonalities and strengths as they work as a team to explore what is important, a goal that students have recognized by describing Sewak in the yearbook as a teacher who makes all incoming ninth graders feel welcome.

Moving from a Deficit Lens to an Asset-Based Lens

There are too many heartbreaking stories of ELL students who are ignored, stigmatized, or underserved in their secondary schools. How we think about the presence of ELL students in our ELA classes makes a difference. When we shift from seeing ELLs through a deficit lens and instead recognize the assets they bring to a classroom, we can begin to find ways to improve our teaching and the learning of all our students.

Deficit lenses are not always obvious; rather, they manifest in multiple ways. One way is when teachers fall into the trap of seeing difference as deficiency, as something that doesn't belong in our English classes. A preservice teacher in one of my research studies, Zack, demonstrated this when he explained: "Having English language learners would be difficult, a challenge. It would be harder, but I guess there's another department for them."

Deficit lenses also arise when we see ourselves as language gatekeepers who must point out the "deficient" language use of students as part of our job—despite research that suggests the position of English teachers as all-knowing experts about language can cause anxiety and actually prevent teachers from implementing a more generative, student-affirming approach (McBee Orzulak, 2012, 2013). This is even more often the case when dealing with ELL students.

Finally, we may be blindsided by what we don't know or don't see in our classrooms, by the assumptions we make about who is a language learner and who is not and by what it means to be a language learner. Student teacher Lindsey explained: "My biggest surprise during parent-teacher conferences was learning that two additional students spoke a language other than English at home."

As ELA teachers, we can work to avoid these three problem areas that keep us from using an asset-based pedagogy with ELL students, a pedagogy that focuses on the strengths and abilities these students bring to the classroom. This book provides resources to help us unpack these misunderstandings of language and

1. Avoid seeing language difference as a problem
2. Avoid taking on the role of language gatekeeper
3. Avoid ignoring the presence of linguistic diversity

Better understanding language can help us avoid these problem areas and reframe curricular challenges into positive steps for improving our ELA classrooms.

What Mainstream Teachers Need to Know: Advice from a District ELL Coordinator

Eliana, who serves as district ELL coordinator, describes what she most wishes mainstream teachers knew about teaching ELL students:

> The number one idea I wish teachers knew about English language learners is that they have great potential to be successful with the appropriate supports in place. Although they may not necessarily be able to demonstrate their abilities in a sophisticated way, . . . it does not mean that they do not have sophisticated ideas.
>
> These students have unique and diverse experiences and perspectives that they can draw upon to make meaningful contributions to a school community. What they don't need is to be pitied, have their hands held at every turn, or have lower standards of achievement or lower expectations applied to them. That will not help them in the long run. It will not help them to access opportunities in the future beyond the K–12 school experience. Teachers must focus on what will prepare [ELL students] for their future and what they need to do to support them in achieving at the highest levels. And as for the parents of ELs, what they want is what every parent wants—for their child to be happy and to succeed.

Varied Dimensions of Strengths: What We Know about ELL Students

We know from the work of scholars focused on how schools best work with ELL students that a positive approach matters (e.g., Soltero, 2011). Our schools need to affirm the value of ELLs and use their home culture and language as assets. To do so, we need to continue language support in mainstream classrooms. We need to understand the range of ELLs in our classrooms and how to engage this diversity of ELL students in rigorous learning in heterogeneous classrooms.

First, we have to better understand the spectrum of experiences ELL students bring to our classrooms, as they do not fit a single profile. As preservice teacher Zack describes and as some of us have assumed, "Aren't English language learners the students who are in the ESL room down the hall?" It is true that some districts define *English learners* or *ELs* as students who qualify for isolated programs due to language learning needs (e.g., Illinois, where I teach, is one of these states). The reality is that the official numbers of language learners do not always reflect the current multilingual reality of our classrooms, as there are different metrics for determining which students are considered "ELL" or "LTELL" or "LEP" or any number of acronyms that have been used to identify language learners; and this official number, based on limited tests, often doesn't reflect the complex picture of which students are still learning English reading, writing, speaking, or listening skills—skills that develop at different speeds and in different ways. Taking one picture of one row of the produce section in a grocery store, for example, will not tell you the whole story about the vegetables available at that store. Similarly, language learning tests offer only a snapshot of the language knowledge of any given student.

The reality is that the US population continues to change rapidly. As the *NCTE Position Paper on the Role of English Teachers in Educating English Language Learners (ELLs)* notes, the growing number of linguistically diverse students already affects our classes and will continue to do so. The next generations will reflect the potential for increased linguistic diversity in the United States. Americans have an exciting opportunity to catch up with our global neighbors in terms of language learning by helping to shift the US population to a majority of multilingual, globally-savvy language users rather than proudly monolingual isolationists.

Since even native speakers continue to learn English throughout their lives, defining *ELL* and what it means to be an English language learner is complicated. Shifting definitions, by various stakeholders, for English proficiency "levels" create challenges for defining what it means to be classified in this way. Again, ELL students bring a spectrum of experiences to the classroom rather than a single profile, and there are many factors that lead to this diversity; social class, geographic origin, educational background, race/ethnicity, and cultural background all factor into students' identities, as I discuss further in Chapter 3.

The constantly shifting terminology and alphabet soup of acronyms can be one of the challenges facing us as we work to better understand teaching in linguistically diverse classrooms. While not everyone will agree with the definitions for all the terms describing English language learners, the authors of the Principles in Practice strand on teaching ELLs (of which this book is a part) collaborated to compile a streamlined Statement of Terminology and Glossary, one that reflects the most current terms and definitions by a group of us who are heavily steeped in the research and practice surrounding linguistic diversity. We offer this list (see pp. xx–xxii) with caution, as we are well aware that terminology describing students—and their language use—often reflects power dynamics. It is easy for terminology to reflect a deficit or exclusionary perspective. The multiple, evolving terms reflect the complexities of language, identity, and academic literacy. Different terminology has been used over time by different stakeholders and has evolved based on demographic shifts, deepening understandings of language, and more complex descriptions of students' use of language. As the *English Journal* column "Lingua Anglia" notes, it's important that we consider moving beyond deficit terminology; the author suggests using the term *multilingual learner* in order to describe students in an asset-based manner (Hickey, 2015).

Even though this imprint strand uses *English language learning* students, or ELL students, to refer to a broad spectrum of students, the question of what terminology do/should we use and why is one that we continue grappling with as we learn more about language in our classrooms. I remind myself that the goal is not necessarily to find the perfect label. Although accurate and precise descriptions of our students and their language use can matter, what is more important are the underlying messages reflected in those labels or terminology. The point of terminology, after all, is to help us understand, support, and affirm our students and their language use.

Next Steps: Better Understanding the Benefits of Language Understandings and the Presence of ELL Students

This book is designed to help mainstream English teachers like you explore the ways understanding language can build your repertoire as an effective teacher of all students. No matter what labels might (or might not) apply to your students, we want all of them to learn savvy ways for using language and engaging in the study of English language arts. The reality is that best practice for teaching ELL students can actually provide benefits for all students. Furthermore, understanding this reality can help us justify both new and tried-and-true ELA methods to our stakeholders, including administrators, parents or guardians, and other teachers.

To do so, in this book you and I together will explore "understanding language," or key notions that help us create responsive classrooms that prioritize respect and rigor. Specifically, we explore how mainstream ELA teachers might begin to understand language in new ways to benefit both ELL and non-ELL students housed in the same classroom.

As a starting place, I discuss supportive teaching resources to help unpack the opportunities inherent in having ELL students and recognizing their strengths in your classroom. The book addresses responses to common curricular challenges to help you get started as you consider how key language understandings can provide support for (1) structuring positive environments for students as both learners and adolescents; (2) providing a language focus in our teaching; and (3) assessing the range of ELL students.

This book provides a series of entry points into the *NCTE Position Paper on the Role of English Teachers in Educating English Language Learners* (from here on referred to as the *NCTE Position Paper*), a document that encourages ELA teachers to acknowledge research in language acquisition and support for multilingual students. I focus on the position paper's description of *knowing students*, *teaching language and content*, and *teaching literacy* (reading and writing), as outlined in Chapter 2. Understanding these areas can help us create classrooms that harness ELA's potential to offer all students key literacy/language skills (reading, writing, and speaking). The principles also support important mindsets and approaches, such as critical, inquiry-based, and multicultural approaches.

The book's goal is to highlight how teachers can create rich, safe ELA classroom environments for ELL students alongside other students in the mainstream classroom by exploring an overarching question: *How do we understand language in order to create rigorous, responsive classroom environments that value ELL students?* Across the chapters, we'll look at strategies for supporting linguistically diverse students in mainstream ELA classrooms that prioritize both respect and rigor. As part of answering this question in a tangible way, the book offers examples of how effective teachers incorporate the cultural and linguistic knowledge of their students to put the principles of respect and rigor into practice as they

- Structure peer-to-peer groups
- Encourage class participation
- Create opportunities for authentic literacy learning and language use
- Select texts and plan units
- Assess student learning and teaching practice

We'll look at research and examples from practice to help regular secondary English teachers support ELL students. We'll also consider specific ways to teach reading and writing that engage all students while supporting ELLs.

For example, Chapter 2 further describes how a responsive approach is one that notices and understands the strengths of ELL students and uses their presence to guide respectful and rigorous instruction for all students as we unpack our own cultural and linguistic expectations. Chapter 3 explores the role of discourse in developing positive relationships in classroom spaces, because creating responsive environments with a range of students helps to extend possibilities for critical thinking and literacy. These understandings of responsive classroom discourses help us counteract deficit discourses related to ELL students through our "mainstream" or "regular" classrooms if they provide spaces for valuing ELL students rather than marginalizing them. You will also learn ways to structure positive environments for students as both learners and adolescents, and to position them as visibly contributing community members. You will read examples of how teacher-student relationships can affirm student identities as part of an approach to supporting language learning.

Because of the wide range of students who could classify as ELL in our mainstream classes, we have a responsibility and challenge to better understand that range and what shifts in instruction might be necessary. That's one reason Chapters 4, 5, and 6 focus on how to use principles of respect and rigor to help us respond to curricular challenges we face in planning instruction and assessment for the range of ELL students in our classrooms. Chapter 4 explores how understandings of varied language demands and resources (i.e., oral, written, academic, and social) help us support language learning and encourage active participation in our literacy communities. Chapter 5 describes how to use our understandings of multilingual learners to better support students in rigorous, responsive reading communities, with attention to how we frame and select texts, scaffold active engagement with those texts, and pair reading and writing tasks. Chapter 6 affirms ways to use assessment productively to communicate high expectations for all students by prioritizing authentic assessment through shared discourses, formative assessment, self-assessment, multiple assessments, and teacher inquiry.

The book also offers ways to build a bridge between stakeholders in your classroom, school, and community contexts. Considering the needs of ELL students can provide us with opportunities to promote better community engagement and collaboration with others, as discussed in Chapter 7.

Getting Started: Questions to Ask Yourself

Considering an Asset-Based Perspective

- What are the strengths of our ELL students?
- What opportunities are available in a multilingual classroom?
- What have you learned from your ELL students
    - about language?
    - about culture?
    - about learning?
    - about yourself?
- What asset-based terms can you use to refer to your ELL students and the process of language learning?

Chapter Two

Respect and Rigor in the Responsive Classroom

Mainstream teachers who are successful in teaching English Learners are those who see the value of learning multiple languages, as opposed to viewing these students as having a deficit to overcome or a problem that must be managed. Teachers who view [ELL students] as bringing skills, knowledge and experience that are assets to the learning environment and to their own personal and academic development are able to see beyond what less successful teachers might consider as extra work on their plate with regard to getting students to meet standards, and demonstrate achievement through various measurable outcomes.

Successful teachers do not resent [ELL students] because of their unique academic needs, but rather embrace the opportunity to utilize their linguistic and cultural knowledge to their advantage, capitalizing on students' strengths. Other characteristics of effective teachers for English learners include creating a warm, nurturing learning environment. Students need to feel cared for and safe, and they need to know that they are valued in order to feel comfortable in the classroom. Teachers should take the time to listen to students and to get to know them.

—Eliana, district ELL coordinator

What Eliana describes here is the need for responsive classrooms for ELL students, which requires teachers who understand and draw on language as a resource to create an affirming environment. Responsive ELA classrooms are both respectful and rigorous environments for our ELL students. As a teacher, you may have questions about this approach, the same questions that some ELA teachers I've talked with have had: Is it fair to change my mainstream ELA class based on the needs of a few multilingual learners? Is it my responsibility to make changes only if I have a high number of ELLs? And if I do want to make changes, where do I start?

Key Understanding: **Responsive ELA classrooms = culturally affirming spaces where linguistically responsive teachers apply their language understandings in order to operationalize principles of respect and rigor in their classroom communities.**

In this chapter, I suggest that making changes in your classroom based on language understandings is more than fair—it is beneficial for all students. Your approach may vary depending on the makeup of your classroom, but certain underlying principles of respect and rigor can help create a more responsive space for all students, not just multilingual ones.

Creating an ELA Oasis: Principles for Building Responsive Classrooms

Our ELA classrooms have special potential to be supportive and vital learning spaces for English language learning (ELL) students. At the same time, ELL students offer a rich addition to our classrooms—when they can be positioned as contributors—especially because of their understandings of language and culture.

What would happen if we constructed our ELA classrooms as oases for ELL (and all) students? By creating a truly responsive classroom, we can establish such an oasis—a safe, productive learning environment. My teaching experiences in a range of schools with diverse groups of students have led me to understand the connection between a responsive approach to teaching and a safety net for all students. Being responsive means understanding the opportunities of the presence of ELL students and then using their presence to guide instruction in ways that can benefit all students.

Why are our ELA classrooms perfectly poised to be an oasis for our ELL students? In short, because of our focus on language. As English language arts teachers, we bring crucial expertise and understand learning standards related to language use: reading, writing, speaking, and listening. Furthermore, ELA classrooms have much potential to be dialogic, address critical pedagogy, explore cultural understandings, and provide nurturing social contexts. These are all qualities that research suggests support multilingual students (e.g., see Case, 2015; Faltis & Wolfe, 1999).

However, to do so, we have to make sure we're not just pontificating about the language arts, but rather asking our students to engage in active reading, writing, speaking, and listening in some particular ways.

Overarching Principles: Respect and Rigor

How do we create the kinds of responsive classrooms that see ELLs as assets and not deficits? How can we use an ELA focus on reading and writing to encourage students' growth in literacy? And how can we do this in a way that helps all students? Two overarching principles of respect and rigor support this kind of work:

- Create respectful classroom contexts.
- Use language as a resource for rigorous learning.

Why Do Respect and Rigor Matter?

Stories of ELL students being underserved continue to emerge in the news. Unfortunately, in some classrooms ELL students may be ostracized or bullied at worst and ignored at best. This negative continuum of how ELL students are treated needs to be counteracted with a positive continuum of acknowledgment, value, respect, and appreciation for their contributions to our ELA classrooms (see Figure 2.1). This positive continuum requires us to have certain understandings about language in order to see or *acknowledge* what students bring to the table—a first step before we can then *value* their contributions, offer and encourage *respect* for linguistic diversity, and even instill deep *appreciation* for linguistic diversity in all of our students.

Figure 2.1. A positive continuum for interacting with English language learners.

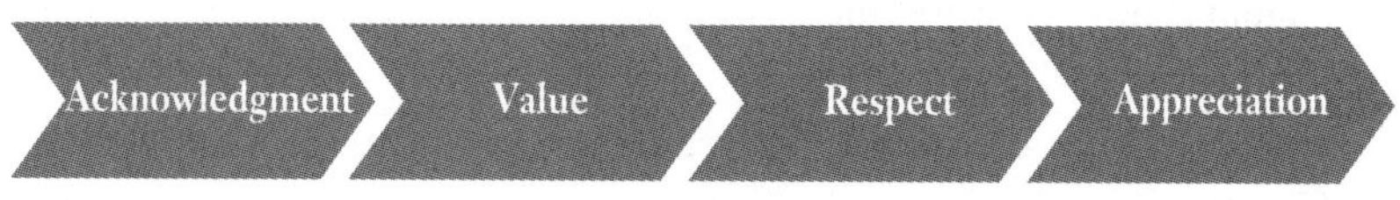

As I discuss throughout the book, responsive classrooms that foster respect and rigor require knowledge of language. The *NCTE Position Paper* focuses on the knowledge and skills *teachers* need in order to serve the literacy needs of ELL students. Multiple scholars have already noted the importance of recognizing what linguistically diverse students offer in the classroom, such as "funds of knowledge," or assets and prior knowledge they bring from their home and communities (see, for instance, Moll & Gonzalez, 1994). According to NCTE's Conference on English Education, "Students bring funds of knowledge to their learning communities, and, recognizing this, teachers and teacher educators must incorporate this knowledge and experience into classroom practice" (2005). As part of this understanding, we need to respect our learners as people who have culturally defined identities.

This means that if we seek to have responsive ELA classrooms, the first principle, creating respectful classroom contexts, is inextricably linked to the second, using language as a resource for rigorous learning. In Table 2.1, I suggest how these two overarching principles connect to the key recommendations of the *NCTE Position Paper*, focusing on (1) knowing students; (2) teaching language and content; and (3) teaching literacy (reading and writing) (page references in the table and elsewhere in the book map to the *NCTE Position Paper* reprinted in the front matter). Understanding language remains key to guiding our choices and discourse in classrooms, which involves planning for ways to use language as a resource so that we can create responsive ELA classrooms.

Imagining Responsive ELA Classrooms: Respect and Rigor in Linguistically Responsive Teaching and Culturally Affirming Environments

The *NCTE Position Paper* considers how our knowledge and skills can be extended in ways that engage ELL students to improve academic achievement and avoid perpetuating what the media often refers to as "educational gaps" facing ELL students. If you're like me, the overarching principles of respect and rigor may seem obvious, something we would all agree with. But less obvious is how to put these principles into practice. What might a classroom look like that is dually focused on respect and rigor, especially for ELLs? In the coming pages, you'll meet many teachers and view classroom vignettes—descriptions of teachers putting the principles into practice—that provide illustrations of the principles. Short vignettes are drawn from the perspectives and experiences of teachers from a broad span of middle and high schools in urban, rural, and suburban areas. In varied populations and contexts, the principles can manifest both similarly and differently.

Table 2.1. Creating Responsive ELA Classrooms: Two Overarching Principles of Respect and Rigor—Principle 1: Create Respectful Classroom Contexts; Principle 2: Use Language as a Resource for Rigorous Learning

Overarching Principles of Respect and Rigor: Applying the NCTE Position Paper		
NCTE Position Paper Categories	**Skills and Knowledge**	**Principles in Practice: Respect and Rigor**
Knowing Students	· Understand the complexity and heterogeneity of ELL students · Understand multiple "teacher-learner" relationships: ∘ "involvement between teachers and students around subject matter and language and literacy proficiency in both languages"(p. xiii) ∘ "adult-child" relationships: "more personal and should include the family" [e.g., provide bridges between home and school] (p. xiii)	*Principle 1: Create respectful classroom contexts.* · Noticing students, knowing about students · Understanding links between language and identity · Debunking language and cultural myths (e.g., helping all class members unpack internalized "ideals" and assumptions about language use) · Understanding how culture plays a part in learning (e.g., provide modeling for all students) *Principle 2: Use language as a resource for rigorous learning.* · How do students want to expand their language understandings? · Who are they as literate people? · Understanding first and additional languages and/or language variation
Teaching Language and Content	· "Providing authentic opportunities to use language in a nonthreatening environment" (p. xiii) · "Teaching text- and sentence-level grammar" in the context of various content areas (p. xiii) · "Teaching the specific features of language students need to communicate in social as well as academic contexts" (p. xiii)	*Principle 1: Create respectful classroom contexts.* · Providing modeling (e.g., think-alouds) and classroom structures to support respectful peer-to-peer interactions *Principle 2: Use language as a resource for rigorous learning.* · Understanding language change · Analyzing language quirks with students · Comparing language use across contexts (e.g., literary texts versus everyday speech) · Planning for language and content objectives; acknowledging academic and social language demands
Teaching Literacy (Reading and Writing)	Reading · "Introducing classroom reading materials that are culturally relevant" using varied themes and difficulty that support students (p. xiv) · "Connecting the readings with the students' background knowledge and experiences" (p. xiv) · "Encouraging students to discuss the readings, including the cultural dimensions of the text" (p. xiv) · "Teaching language features, such as text structure, vocabulary, and text- and sentence-level grammar to facilitate comprehension of the text" (p. xiv) · "'Front loading' comprehension via a walk through the text or a preview of the main ideas, and other strategies that prepare students for the topic of the text" (e.g., provide opportunities to read a more accessible text first) (p. xiv) Writing · "Encouraging contributions from all students, and promoting peer interaction to support learning" (p. xv) · "Designing writing assignments for a variety of audiences, purposes, and genres, and scaffolding the writing instruction" (p. xv) · Glossing and "providing models of well-organized papers for the class" (p. xv) · "Making comments explicit and clear (both in written response and in oral responses)," and using feedback to address both global and local concerns (p. xv)	*Principle 1: Create respectful classroom contexts.* · Understanding the role of engagement and motivation · Choosing strategically when to correct; understanding correction's limited value · Encouraging creativity *Principle 2: Use language as a resource for rigorous learning.* · Addressing in/formal language differences · Creating a language-rich environment · Building on what students know · Not delaying writing and reading experiences · Teaching processes of writing for all, providing time to marinate · Providing focused feedback · Considering differences and connections between language demands in reading and writing activities · Thinking aloud to model and frame reading and writing processes

Background for Overarching Principles of Respect and Rigor

Before moving on, let's discuss how these principles of respect and rigor that shape responsive classrooms are based on scholars' past descriptions of *linguistically responsive teaching* (Lucas & Villegas, 2011) and the ways responsive teachers create *culturally affirming environments* (Nieto, 2000).

Considering our role as teachers can help us shape the classroom environment to create affirming spaces. Understanding ourselves as linguistically responsive teachers who can create culturally affirming environments leads us to provide ELL students with nonbiased spaces for ELA learning that privilege respect, high expectations, and rigorous learning opportunities. As Eliana notes in the chapter opening, to do this effectively, we need asset-based views and language understandings that help us shape and create nurturing, responsive spaces for students.

Respect and Rigor: What Does Responsive ELA Teaching Look Like in Practice?

Linguistically Responsive Teaching: Teachers' Orientations to Promote Respect and Rigor

Linguistically responsive teaching (LRT) (Lucas & Villegas, 2011) promotes positive teaching that draws on asset metaphors, rather than reactive teaching that casts ELL students as a challenge or disruption to the mainstream classroom. An increasing number of teachers have taken on this asset-based approach to how they respond to ELL students in their classrooms, recognizing the importance of connecting language understandings to respect. What does it mean to be a linguistically responsive teacher, according to this research by Lucas and Villegas? These teachers have

- A *sociolinguistic consciousness*, or the "understanding of the connection between language, culture, and identity," as well as the "sociopolitical dimensions of language use and language education" (p. 57)
- Orientations of *value for linguistic diversity* and the *advocacy for English language learners*
- Abilities to learn about students' "backgrounds, experiences, proficiencies"; identify "language demands of classroom tasks"; apply "key principles of second language learning"; and scaffold instruction (p. 57)

In practice, these characteristics lead teachers to make sure that ELL students have opportunities to be visibly contributing classroom members. Responsive teachers who value linguistic diversity and advocate for ELLs are able to do so because they are engaged in an ongoing process of understanding both their students' backgrounds and proficiencies as well as the language demands of different aspects of their ELA coursework. Increasing our own complex knowledge of language is a key element; linguistically responsive teachers recognize their responsibility to consider how their language understandings shape their teaching. As the positive continuum suggests, to fully provide the respect and rigor needed in our classrooms, it's our responsibility to value, advocate, understand, and learn about language. LRT emphasizes this teacher role.

A linguistically responsive approach to teaching matters. A responsive approach helps teachers avoid marginalizing the growing linguistically diverse population of students and contributing to declines in achievement these students often experience in middle and high school. Creating classrooms conducive to learning for ELL students can in turn lead to richer, more supportive environments for all students, as all students grapple with learning academic language. But to do so, we must make sure we consider our role as teachers, reflect on our past experiences as language users, and use knowledge about language in our teaching.

Culturally Affirming Environment: Creating Spaces for Respect and Rigor in the Classroom

In turn, linguistically responsive teachers apply their language understandings to how they shape the classroom environment and use this knowledge to shape an affirming environment (see Table 2.2). Your classroom, or entire school, can serve as a culturally affirming environment (Nieto, 2000). Central to Nieto's broad conceptual framework for multicultural education, the concept of "culturally affirming environment" can help us provide the safe, nurturing place Eliana suggests for ELL students in the ELA classroom. This environment needs to be a nonracist, nonbiased space for learning that privileges

- Affirmation and respect (e.g., through discourses used)
- Shared understanding that all students have talents and strengths
- Language as a resource
- Interpersonal connections (peer-peer; student-teachers; school-family and community members)

This understanding of the environment also means considering the curricular resources and materials used in the classroom and the overall school environment. To create such a space, teachers (and the school) must hold high expectations, select materials purposefully, and offer rigorous learning opportunities. For instance, understanding students' language assets enables teachers to more objectively evaluate students' ability levels, rather than make baseless, uninformed assumptions about what students already *can* do and what they *can't* do. It also means providing all students with social and cultural capital, such as access to

Table 2.2. Moving toward Responsive ELA Classrooms: Key Understandings to Promote Respect and Rigor

Understanding Self: Using Self and Language Understandings	**Understanding Students:** Gaining Knowledge of ELL Students	**Understanding Contexts:** Shaping Affirming Spaces with Understandings	**Understanding ELA Curricula:** Applying Understandings
Teacher:	Teacher:	Teacher:	Teacher:
Considers assumptions (asset and deficit metaphors); draws on assets Learns from past experiences with language demands; linguistic diversity Learns about students' backgrounds (language, culture, identity, ability levels) Values linguistic diversity Advocates for affirming spaces in environment (classroom, school, community) Identifies language demands; knows key language principles	Acknowledges range of "ELL" students and limits of definitions: *"EL"* *"Generation 1.5"* *"ESL"* *"ELL"* *"multilingual"* *"SIFE" (students with interrupted formal education)* Acknowledges students' goals and varied proficiencies	Considers range of contexts influencing language learning: *Classroom* *School* *Neighborhood* *State* *United States* Understands how these contexts are shaped by *Definitions* *Testing* *Supports* *Beliefs* Creates culturally affirming spaces through actions: ✓ Communicates need for nonbiased, nonthreatening spaces ✓ Uses and teaches discourses affirming linguistic diversity ✓ Fosters supportive interpersonal, peer-to-peer connections ✓ Creates language-rich environment that values multiple languages ✓ Offers culturally relevant texts and materials ✓ Designs assignments that draw on and support multiple language resources ✓ Builds bridges between home and school ✓ Addresses language myths, such as there's only one form of English used in all contexts ✓ Values and supports social and academic language use	Builds on students' language resources Includes rigorous learning opportunities; communicates high expectations Includes active, participatory literacy learning Develops appreciation for linguistic diversity Attends to language demands in reading, writing, speaking, and listening Values curricular links between language and culture

varied understandings of and perspectives on US education, society, and culture. For instance, as discussed in Chapter 5, teachers consider language in text selection and framing, the setup of activities, and assignment criteria; they consider both how their choices build on students' assets and how their choices provide new, rigorous learning experiences for students. These factors contribute to an empowering and just environment—one that benefits all (Nieto, 1999). Creating culturally affirming environments as a linguistically responsive teacher means understanding language's link to culture. Operationalizing this link between language and culture in our classrooms provides the potential to explore multiple perspectives, break down stereotypes, and discourage dangerous ideologies of xenophobia.

Steps toward Connecting Respect and Rigor to Build Responsive Classrooms

How do responsive teachers create a climate of respect and rigor in their classrooms? Let's consider three steps in relation to our understandings about our students, our contexts, and our curriculum:

1. Considering Respect and Rigor in Relation to Learning about Students

Like me, you may recognize that it's hard to know what you don't know about language. Sometimes our limited knowledge and expectations get in the way of knowing how to express respect or to create a responsive environment. Sometimes our lack of knowledge leads us to not understand where students are coming from. For instance, "Without such an understanding [about linguistics], teachers sometimes assume that there is something wrong with students whose ways of using language are not what they expect" (Adger, Snow, & Christian, 2002, p. 10).

Responsive teachers look closely to better understand their students' contributions. They realize that ELL students are a complex, heterogeneous group. It's essential for us to gain knowledge about this complexity in order to set up rigorous learning. Responsive teachers consider the contexts, stereotypes, and realities that may attempt to cast these contributions as a problem or deficit. This means noticing the diversity of our students' motivations, abilities, and personalities.

For example, one responsive teacher notices that while many of his language-learning students can bring tenacity to classroom tasks, some may need more support. Another teacher comments that while ELL students are often eager learners and hungry for knowledge (often depicted as the stereotypical hardworking seeker of the "American Dream"), some care more about being well-rounded teens. Other teachers note that many language learners they encounter are optimistic, mature, and/or have a strong work ethic. The next chapter talks more about the varied social, educational, and

The Responsive ELA Classroom: Considering Your Students

How Do You Get to Know Your Students?

Think about: what methods do you already use to get to know your students?

Take note: what methods could you add to gain better understanding of your ELL students?

- Beginning of the year surveys
- Anecdotes from other teachers
- Team planning across disciplines
- Testing data
- Family conferences
- Introductory writing prompts
- Informal conversations before class
- Community oral histories
- Video documentaries of community life
- Whole-class or small-group discussions

cultural factors you may uncover as you consider ways to get to know your ELL students. For now, take a look at "Considering Your Students" in the sidebar on page 26 to see if you can identify ways you've found to unpack the diversity of students in your class, or if this list sparks new ideas you could use as you get to know students in the future.

2. Considering Respect and Rigor in School Context(s)

Like me, you probably seek to create a respectful ELA classroom environment. Especially when we work with ELL students, however, developing a new focus on understanding language in relation to the larger classroom and school contexts is vital. We need to have some key language understandings in order to fully create an equitable environment that supports respectful, rigorous learning.

Because the population of ELL students is diverse and complex, responsive teachers ask many questions to better understand the specific students in their classroom and school contexts. This is particularly important in terms of language use as we seek to understand the connection between language and current assumptions, discourses, and climates for learning that might shape our teaching. In the end, the language understandings that create responsive ELA classrooms must start with us and then become a key part of how we in turn shape our classroom and larger school environments. Thus, being a responsive teacher means understanding how language can and should affect our pedagogy and shape how we set up the classroom environment. It also means we may need to engage in advocacy to help align the larger contexts, such as school, district, and national policies, with the environment in our own classrooms.

3. Considering Respect and Rigor in the ELA Curriculum

As a teacher who cares about your students, you recognize that there's never a one-size-fits-all approach to supporting learning; therefore, the curriculum needs to reflect the dynamics of the students in our classes. Responsive teachers also consider how an ELA curriculum provides ways for ELL students to contribute to the classroom environment through opportu-

The Responsive ELA Classroom: Considering Your Contexts

Think about: your current context—classroom, school, workplace, university, or other educational context. What do you already know?

- What are the current resources for supporting ELL students? What is needed (e.g., policies, awareness, support staff)?
- What do you know about language learning and the school population?
    - Population numbers
    - Variety of languages spoken
    - Variety of English(es) in prior education
    - Variety of cultures represented
    - Complexity of Spanish-speaking population (e.g., varied subgroups)
    - Ratios between groups
    - Educational background
    - Stereotypes, attitudes, or deficit beliefs

The Responsive ELA Classroom: Considering the ELA Curriculum

Think about: how do you apply language understandings in teaching? For instance, consider a unit you've taught recently.

- How was language learning integrated throughout the unit?
- What kinds of social interactions were included and how was language considered in these interactions?
    - Writing
    - Speaking
    - Listening
    - Reading
- How did this unit's text selections and reading and writing activities build on students' cultural and language backgrounds, experiences, and proficiencies?
    - How did these selections and activities help promote a respectful classroom context?
    - How did these selections and activities draw on students' language use as a resource?

nities for individual inquiry, active and collaborative learning, and knowledge construction.

Curriculum connections to larger cultural contexts can matter greatly. For instance, a responsive teacher might design an inquiry project that calls on notions of courage in different cultures. While reading stories from multiple backgrounds that serve as both cultural windows and mirrors, the class might explore questions like *What does it mean to be courageous?* Or, as Faltis and Coulter (2008) describe, a class might look at cultural understandings of beauty. In this class, students could share experiences, read texts, and question the ways understandings of beauty are shaped by cultural norms, explaining, for instance, how media representations shape understandings by offering only limited forms of physical beauty, compared to a wider range appreciated in different cultures. In Chapter 5, we see a teacher's example of this kind of curricular work using an anthropological lens to explore notions of culture in relation to the study of *Things Fall Apart* and other literature.

Considering Respect and Rigor: Our Experiences and Assumptions as ELA Teachers

ELA Teachers as Language Police or as Allies

As responsive ELA teachers, we learn how to analyze assumptions about English language use as we learn about students, shape our classroom contexts, and design curricula. Beyond lack of knowledge about language and/or ELL students, we can face obstacles based on deeply ingrained language beliefs in US culture. English teachers are sometimes perceived as language police by others; we've probably all had people cover their mouths and say, "Oh, I'll have to watch my grammar" when they find out what you do for a living. On the flipside, we have the opportunity to cast ourselves as allies in the language learning journey—we are often seen as a knowledgeable support for those eager to know more about language.

Many of us are native English speakers and may be able to mark all language "errors" based on our sense of "standard" English (though scholars have noted that these conceptions of a standard are often in flux and idiosyncratic). However, many experienced teachers of ELL students have noted that the "language police" position is not a generative one (which I've also confirmed in my own experience and research [Godley, Carpenter, & Werner, 2007; McBee Orzulak, 2012, 2013; Schleppegrell & Go, 2007; Scott, Straker, & Katz, 2009; Wiley & Lukes, 1996]). As these experienced teachers of multilingual classrooms explain, it's more useful to focus on meaning and thinking rather than on correction in their approach to teaching writing:

> I have figured out, by the way, what's important. . . . I would just rather that [students] have a meaningful sentence with the wrong preposition than a sentence with a perfect preposition and no meaning. I mean you pick your battles.
>
> If you want your students to think, you shouldn't be correcting them. Let them think. Let them develop their thoughts because if you start prescribing rules, then they will be thinking about the correctness of their speech and they will not be developing their ideas.

This focus on meaning doesn't suggest that teachers don't pay attention to language patterns or instruction (see Chapters 4 and 5). In fact, scholars (Charity Hudley & Mallinson, 2011; Lippi-Green, 2012) note that teachers need a better understanding of language variation (i.e., the sociolinguistic consciousness supported by linguistically responsive teaching). This sociolinguistic, linguistically responsive perspective can actually help us as we consider the language of all of our students, including those who are "bidialectal" or just adjusting their English language use (social and academic) to adapt to new social or academic contexts.

Responsive ELA Teachers: Knowing Students and Respecting Language Variety

Ruth, an experienced ELA high school teacher, describes her approach to language variation as opposed to a colleague's response:

> I can remember a colleague of mine, a white colleague of mine, when a student came in speaking calmly and respectfully but in [African American English] the teacher just getting red in the face and saying, "That's not English. You won't speak that in this classroom."
>
> [I was just] appalled because by then I had had this amazing professional development through the International Reading Association by Rebecca Wheeler, the linguist. And I had been actually using code-switching in the classroom and having kids sort of translate between an [African American English] version of a phrase and a school English version of a phrase.

So why are we talking about language variation in a book about ELLs? In part, because the discussion surrounding phrases such as "Standard English learners" and "That's not English" remain problematic whether a student is a speaker of a language variety (like African American English) or of another language. I'm not trying to obscure the achievement gaps between some language learners and their monolingual white and/or African American counterparts. However, the need for

Considering Perspectives about English: Which English Is Better? What Is "Real" English?

Language use of different kinds can trigger passionate reactions, and these reactions are often based in deeply internalized beliefs about English language, whether these different kinds of English are connected to online, social, cultural, or regional contexts. Global versions of English complicate our teaching of English in a US context. Further, power is inherent in debates about what counts as English.

One area to explore with students is the ways variations of English can be portrayed in relation to beliefs about people. ELL students who have studied English in other countries can sometimes speak to global perceptions and understandings of English, and they may bring their own beliefs about "better" English to the classroom. All students who have consumed US culture have some knowledge about how language can be linked to identity. Here are two cases for you to consider related to language beliefs.

Case 1. A US Perspective: Disney Accents

Lippi-Green (2012) has shown that Disney films often portray "bad characters" through foreign accents and argues that this can teach small children a discriminatory, ethnocentric way of understanding language.

Think about a recent film you've seen. Do the characters speak with accents that perpetuate cultural stereotypes? Are there differences in how British English accents are portrayed versus African American language? You might notice that main characters often speak "mainstream" American or British English, whereas racially or culturally inflected English is often spoken by villains, stereotypical, or second-tier characters. For example, in the film *Aladdin* the heroes speak a fairly "mainstream" American accent, while the bad guys are the ones with "foreign" accents. Sometimes British English accents in Disney films signal a more snobbish or educated character (one who is also sometimes a villain, like *The Lion King*'s Scar, who has a clear British accent even though his good brother speaks with an American English accent).

Case 2. Students from Other Countries: British English Is Real English

Students from other countries sometimes claim that British English is the real "English" (Johnson, 2008) because they have learned British English during their schooling. Have you internalized any beliefs about which form of English is "better"? If you hear English on the BBC, does it sound "smart" to you? If so, what do you think has shaped that belief?

(See Chapter 7 and the annotated bibliography for further resources about language variety and myths.)

language understandings in both situations often intersect: the need to understand different aspects of language use; the need to unpack myths (e.g., beliefs about the superiority of different language uses or beliefs about language learning); the need to draw on students' linguistic and cultural assets rather than assume a deficit; and the need to plan strategically about language demands.

Students bring beliefs about when and how to use English language varieties to classroom activities because English changes in different contexts and over time. For example, students in today's classrooms—whether ELLs or not—frequently intersperse text with other online language, internalizing much of the informal and sometimes multimodal ways of using language (e.g., emoticons and symbols) common in online spaces. Such spaces can offer a unique learning opportunity for ELL students: a moment to use playful language to write the way they speak informally. As teachers we can unpack our assumptions about the kinds of academic discourse we expect to see in those spaces, such as when we ask ELA students to blog, and use those opportunities to introduce ELL students to the shifts in language use that will help them learn academic English.

Next Steps: Respect and Rigor in the Responsive Classroom

The overarching principles linked to the *NCTE Position Paper* remind us that one of the opportunities of having ELL students in our ELA classrooms is that their presence can help us examine our expectations about the role of culture and language in our classrooms. Students help us explore and expand language understandings as we seek to create more respectful, rigorous multicultural and multilingual environments for all to study the English language arts. Assessing our language beliefs, experiences, and assumptions—about students, about English language, about our contexts—all help us become more responsive teachers who can shape an ELA environment that fosters respect and rigor for ELL students.

The next chapter further explores how we structure responsive spaces. We all need to consider our own cultural assumptions and experiences, so reflect on the questions in the sidebar before continuing.

Getting Started: Questions to Ask Yourself as a Responsive Teacher

Considering Your Experiences: Thinking through Who We Are and What We Know

- What cross-cultural experiences have I had?
- What language learning experiences have I had?
- What feelings (positive, negative, or ambivalent) have emerged for me related to language(s) and culture(s) I have experienced?

Considering Your Goals:

- What do I need to know more about?
- What do I need to know about language?
- What are the limits of my understanding?
- How can I expand my understanding of my students' backgrounds?

Classroom Vignettes

Chapter Three

Structuring Responsive Learning Spaces in ELA Classrooms

Diana *excels in her Advanced English class, and her teacher often writes on her papers that her work is meticulous. Diana works hard on editing her papers at home and in the school's writing center because she has a strong desire to be seen as "non-ELL" by her English teacher and classmates. The first time the English class has an in-class written exam, however, Diana needed an extra hour to finish her essays because it often takes her a long time to get her ideas down in writing. Her teacher seemed surprised, saying, "But you speak fine," and going on to comment on the "ESL-type errors" the teacher noted in Diana's in-class writing, such as differences in verb tense. Diana worries that maybe the teacher will treat her differently now. In her large school district, students classified as "ESL" work initially with dedicated ESL staff, so Diana is concerned that she may be separated from the other mainstream students.*

***David** is newly arrived to the United States from a refugee camp in Uganda. He has experienced war-torn situations from a young age that have consistently interrupted his formal schooling. The teacher at his private middle school, where he has been placed directly into the ELA classroom, asked that he mention his own culture in a narrative writing assignment. At first David was excited, but he soon began to feel uncomfortable sharing his stories with peers who make fun of his accent and seem focused on things like the school's football team.*

***Luis** is in what some people call a "silent stage." He sometimes pretends to understand even when he does not. When his teachers ask, "Do you understand?" Luis always says yes. Sometimes his English teacher asks Luis to act out what he is supposed to be doing. As an ELL beginner, Luis appreciates when his teachers use simple language structures and avoid long clauses. He likes his English class because the teacher uses predictable language for classroom routines. His teacher employs the buddy system so that Luis can figure out classroom routines. This is much better than the situation in another class, where Luis had to sit alone in silence waiting for the teacher to have time for him. His English teacher seems to understand that Luis is going to make mistakes and that his overall message is what's important.*

***Vanessa** is slated to be the valedictorian of her high school and grew up in the United States while speaking only Spanish before she entered kindergarten. Her experience with US bilingual education in kindergarten and beyond has inspired her to study elementary education in college and become a bilingual teacher. Many of her teachers have been bilingual and/or have described the value of bilingualism, which has affirmed Vanessa's choice to continue learning in both Spanish and English as she begins her journey to becoming a teacher.*

***Áron** speaks Hungarian at home and attends Hungarian school on the weekends to develop his reading and writing abilities in that language. When he introduced his teacher to his parents at family conferences, the teacher seemed flustered and surprised to find out that he spoke an additional language. "At least you have a language in which to emote," his teacher exclaimed.*

Each of these students represents a different ELL story. And each of the teachers' moves in relation to these students has implications for students' success and engagement in the learning community as a responsive space.

Consider how the students and their stories would shape your interactions in your classroom. How do these portraits represent teachers' understandings (and misunderstandings) of their students? What might you do in each situation? Whether developing our own relationships with students or working to structure effective peer-to-peer relationships, our understanding of our ELL students' multifaceted identities is key to developing a responsive classroom. And if these portraits strike a chord and seem too true, remember this: we all can encounter challenges when we move beyond our limited experiences. For that reason, we need to learn more.

What more do we need to know? Linguist Walt Wolfram reminds us that "educators should have specific knowledge about the community language patterns of their students" (1998, p. 116). The reality is that there can be a wide spectrum of multilingual students in our classes. And with that spectrum, our challenge is to create a responsive community that recognizes multilingual students' strengths and abilities.

The range of ELL students can mean that teachers struggle to notice and identify students' strengths, avoid deficit perspectives, and offer empathy for students' language learning journeys. Given this range, how do we start, from the very first days of a new class of students, to engage with this complexity of student identities in effective ways? How do we avoid assumptions about students' written versus oral language proficiency? How do we ensure that students are comfortable sharing with others? How do we structure classroom interactions to provide opportunities and options for language use? How do we avoid making assumptions about students' academic achievement—as some ELLs will be the best and brightest and others will struggle? How do we avoid racial and cultural assumptions about language use that can obscure understanding students' strengths?

> ***Key Understanding:*** **How we understand discourse about language in our ELA classrooms—how we talk about language and language beliefs; use language; and structure language learning interactions—contributes to our ability to create a responsive learning space for ELL students.**

Considering Our Teaching Interactions: Understanding Language to Develop Community

Creating respectful classroom contexts for learning is crucial because the tenor of our interactions matters. Just as a responsive context supports ELL students, their presence in our classes can help us more purposefully develop an inclusive community of practice that is extended by a variety of student perspectives, contributions to critical thinking, and more complex ways of thinking about literacy.

What does it look like to cultivate a caring, responsive community?

What discourse(s) and language understandings lead to the environment we desire?

Understandings of language shape our classroom environment, as we not only incorporate language related to content, but also use language in relationship with others through our interactions. *Discourse* includes how we talk about language, use language, and structure language learning interactions. We know that the ways we use discourse in interactions can position students as powerful, literate individuals (Rex & Schiller, 2009), whether that discourse is being used by the teacher or other students, inherent in the assignments, or embedded in curricular activities.

Meet Maja: A Focal Teacher

Throughout the next few chapters, extended, in-depth examples of teaching will help us fully unpack how responsive classrooms develop and are maintained. In this chapter, we begin following Maja. Extended depictions of Maja's teaching demonstrate how a teacher can integrate the principles of a responsive classroom into her planning, instruction, and assessment practices in a specific context.

Maja has been teaching English in multiple formats over the past two decades. She teaches—or has taught—various ELA courses, including AP English, "regular" English, and honors-level English. She has a background in Teaching English to Speakers of Other Languages (TESOL) and has taught at neighborhood public schools. Multilingual herself, Maja uses her own language learning experiences to sensitize her to the struggles her students face, as well as the benefits of multilingualism. In the vignettes in this book, we will visit Maja as she teaches mainstream ELA at an urban secondary school that serves as a college preparatory magnet school in a large city. This school includes a population of students from a range of linguistic backgrounds and academic levels. Maja's English language arts classes include large numbers of English language learners, many of whom might be classified as "long-term" ELL or Generation 1.5 students. She also teaches some bidialectal and/or native English-speaking students. In the following vignette, notice how Maja begins to create a responsive classroom community on the first day of school.

This glimpse into Maja's classroom frames this chapter's conversation about how we create responsive classroom contexts by understanding the range of students and their language uses and considering how these affect our choices as we seek to create nurturing relationships among students and between us and our students.

Creating a Responsive Community from Day One

On the first day of the school year, Maja has placed block posters around the room with thought-provoking quotations to help students get into conversation as they begin developing a strong academic community. The quotations are selected from texts students will read that year, such as *The Color of Water, Persepolis, Othello,* and *Things Fall Apart:*

> When I was a boy, I used to wonder where my mother came from, how she got on this earth. When I asked her where she was from, she would say, "God made me," and change the subject. When I asked her if she was white, she'd say, "No. I'm light-skinned," and change the subject again. Answering questions about her personal history did not jibe with Mommy's view of parenting twelve curious, wild, brown-skinned children. She issued orders and her rule was law. Since she refused to divulge details about herself or her past, and because my stepfather was largely unavailable to deal with questions about himself or Ma, what I learned of Mommy's past I learned from my siblings. We traded information on Mommy the way people trade baseball cards at trade shows, offering bits and pieces fraught with gossip, nonsense, wisdom, and sometimes just plain foolishness. "What does it matter to you?" my older brother Richie scoffed when I asked him if we had any grandparents. "You're adopted anyway."—James McBride, *The Color of Water*

> Villain, be sure thou prove my love a whore;
> Be sure of it;
> give me the ocular proof:
> Or by the worth of man's eternal soul,
> Thou hadst been better have been born a dog
> Than answer my waked wrath! —William, Shakespeare, *Othello*

—Marjane Satrapi, *Persepolis*

continued on next page

As students come into the room, they choose a poster that speaks to them for some reason and stand in front of it. Students talk with one other person who has chosen that poster, sharing how their selected quotations connect to "who they are." This icebreaker provides the range of students in her class a starting point for finding commonalities with each other and seeing connections, often across linguistic, gender, ethnic, religious, and other differences. It also begins to develop the academic capital in the class, as students are connecting their experiences to literature and one another, a key understanding developed throughout the year.

Maja knows from experience that many of her students often don't speak unless they feel safe, so starting with a sense of connection and community from day one is key. She ensures that no one makes fun of students with accents, and listens to the pair discussions as she circulates the room. She moderates the discussions informally, standing alongside students as a participant herself, modeling how to use students' names in the conversations, and noting commonalities with enthusiasm. She tries to link to students' sense of fun and life, their loves and passion, instead of how they sound.

Cultivating a Community of Practice: The Key Role of Caring, Interactive Communities

Teachers who put principles of responsive teaching into action are skilled at creating supportive classroom environments. One starting place is to consider our relationships with students. Teacher-student relationships remain a powerful force in the success of ELL students in our ELA classrooms. Dissonance between teachers and students can lead to disengagement (Ortmeier-Hooper, 2013b) and prevent us from reaching all students. Some scholars have suggested that helping teachers have meaningful relationships with ELL students is actually a better use of professional development time than a focus on strategies (Jimenez, Rose, Cole, & Flushman, 2011; Lee, 2005; Valenzuela, 1999). Taking time for meaningful relationships can mean taking responsibility for students and knowing about their lives outside of school. For instance, an *ethic of caring* (Noddings, 2005) can be important in teacher-student relationships: this ethic is developed through affirming the assets of ELLs and supporting authentic dialogue in our classrooms. Maja's opening activity initiates this kind of dialogue. In the student portraits that open this chapter, Luis's teacher also does so by creating a buddy system for a student who is still learning how to participate in the class, rather than letting that student become isolated.

Other scholars have described how creating ways for ELL students to become members of the classroom, conceptualized as a community of practice, can be beneficial to the type of interactive, contributory environment needed for genuine learning (Faltis & Wolfe, 1999). This metaphor of *community of practice* recognizes that ELL students have real contributions to make in our classrooms. It also means recognizing that each community uses specific discourses to signal knowledge; for example, particular ways of speaking and writing are used to communicate academic understandings, and ELL students need to be able to help shape and access those discourses.

What does it look like for a classroom to develop as a responsive community of practice for ELL students? Actions we can take to provide responsive classrooms with ELL students include:

- Offering grade-appropriate, rigorous opportunities for learning, such as making sure ELL students engage with key content and concepts prioritized at the grade level (like suitable analytical or argumentation skills at their ability level but still connected to grade-level ELA standards)
- Integrating language learners into the school environment (and beyond) through school club opportunities, learning structures, and service projects
- Learning about the students in the classroom, avoiding the excuse that there are too many different cultures represented to understand
- Providing means for students to have a voice in developing a safe and welcoming environment—this includes creating a space that is language-rich and values all languages held by students
- Understanding the range of stakeholders and community members who provide supports for ELL students
- Inquiring about families and using family members' names in these conversations
- Advocating against English-only policies in the school
- Realizing that having even one multilingual student in the class provides an opportunity for increased attention to language understandings and classroom discourse

Fostering Positive Teacher-Student Relationships

As described in Maja's first day vignette, teacher-student relationships should be established from the first day of a class because the discourses used to frame classroom interactions signal what is valued in the classroom space. Maja values her ELL students' abilities to collaborate and make personal connections to literature. She also knows that the small-group structures will help her ELL students participate and share with others. This contrasts with how many of the teachers in the opening portraits did not know enough about their students' abilities to build on them in genuine ways or to support their active participation. The point is this: the ways we understand language shape how we approach our students. Creating a positive relationship requires first knowing about their language use and then considering how our teaching moves can both affirm and extend their language use.

Maja describes how she adapts the ways she approaches students based on what she knows about their linguistic and cultural experiences:

> Capitalizing on not only ELLs' but all other students' linguistic experience and knowledge—whether it be code-switching, playing with registers, or comparing languages—as well as building relationships with them is key to good teaching and learning.
>
> Some ELLs and/or their families focus mostly on achievement, so conversations about achievement and success are important.
>
> Some ELLs who have more tenuous family relationships or gaps in education rely on building relationships with their teachers. These ELLs and others who need more emotional support enjoy sharing personal information with their teachers either through journal or narrative writing, "grade defenses" [self-assessment writing, described more in Chapter 6], one-on-one conferences, or daily informal, non-school-related interactions, such as "How was your lunch?" and "How is your grandma?"

Considering who your students are in order to frame your discursive moves, as Maja does, can help you begin to create the interpersonal connections needed to promote rigor in your class.

Encouraging Positive Peer-to-Peer Interactions

Part of the teacher-student relationship requires structuring ways to encourage positive peer-to-peer relationships and identities by creating nonracist, nonbiased spaces. Privileging affirmation and respect requires first modeling these approaches. It also means helping students understand that their peers all have talents and strengths. All students need to have a sense of their social and cultural capital and the knowledge and abilities they bring to the classroom community.

As teachers, we encourage this type of positive peer-to-peer interaction by making sure our classroom communities reflect and value students' varied abilities. For instance, the classroom environment—such as the images displayed, languages used, or student grouping—can shape peers' perceptions of one another and their place in the classroom. How we select and use materials (texts, examples, and student work) also shapes who is perceived as valued (Nieto, 1999). We also shape how students interact with one another through the ways we address cultural myths and related language beliefs.

Ethnocentrism, or the inability to understand cultures outside one's own, can cause student relationships to break down. Cross-cultural communication challenges may occur, as verbal and nonverbal communication intersect with cultural knowledge. Additionally, some multilingual students may go through stages of cultural accommodation that includes periods of cultural shock that can lead to frustration with a new culture. David, in the opening portraits, is one example, as he struggles with encountering peers who seem focused on trivial social events like football games rather than on devastating global events like those he has experienced. Having a range of students in our classrooms helps us to encourage perspective taking, as students can learn to acknowledge the cultural and linguistic biases they may bring to subject matter or experiences. (For more on culture, see DeCapua and Wintergerst [2004], a resource text that includes many experiential activities related to culture and language.)

How we arrange space in our classrooms can also positively or negatively affect peer-to-peer interaction, as we all know when we move our desks around. However, if students come from a different school environment where arrangements other than rows of desks and the teacher situated at the front of the room might seem unusual, take the time to explain why or how that space is used to foster an interactive, collaborative classroom environment. To develop a community of practice that values reading and writing, we can make sure, when possible, the space reflects those commitments:

- Are there spaces for small-group or pair work as well as large-group and individualized instruction?
- Does the setup encourage students to share their work as readers and writers with one another?
- Does the setup support ELL students who may need to access norms or key ideas during small-group discussions (e.g., access to on-the-wall visuals or reading and writing materials)?
- Does the setup avoid isolating some students from effective peer-to-peer work?

In Practice: Creating a Respectful, Rigorous Environment through Student Contributions and Clear Expectations

Key Practices in This Vignette

- Generating classroom norms with students
- Providing visual reminders for a language-rich environment
- Communicating expectations for successful participation
- Modeling respectful classroom discourse

continued on next page

Part of helping peers value one another requires helping them work together as a whole class to develop norms for that community. In the first days of school, Maja structures her class to create an environment where contributions are expected and valued. She works with students to generate classroom norms that they write on large easel paper and then post around the room. Students often generate and contribute to the classroom content, as Maja creates a language-rich environment that encourages use of student contributions on wall posters, the overhead projector, and even the whiteboard. For example, descriptions of verbal and nonverbal cues for active listening are recorded by students in rainbow-colored marker script and posted around the room for reference points during small- and large-group discussions.

This is just one of the many ways throughout the year that Maja's students share examples, generate class rules, and work through writing revisions, all in ways that contribute to the community—as visuals, as examples, or as evidence of their learning.

In the first days of the of school year, Maja also hands out her whole-class participation rules and rubric, which outline what a student needs to do to be an A or a B student, as well as what a C or a D student looks like. It's an involved handout (see "the Reflective Student Self-Assessment/Whole Class Participation Rubric for Practicing YOUR VOICE on p. 45) that describes the behaviors students are expected to exhibit to be successful. Maja explains some of the rules:

- Acknowledging other students' contributions by name and piggybacking off their contribution
- Pushing back gently on what the other students and the teacher have said

Because students need time to internalize these rules, Maja introduces and reviews them gradually, taking a couple of months to make sure students understand each part. For instance, she has noticed that it takes many students this long to truly understand a statement like "don't dominate" as a way of monitoring their air time; there may be initial misunderstandings when some students think "don't dominate" just means to keep their mouths shut. So Maja points out different options and structures for active, positive contributions and listening. (Note: Since the time in which the activities described in these vignettes took place, Maja has replaced "don't dominate" and "doesn't complain" on her rubric with "monitor air time" based on student feedback. Maja realized that her initial attempt at humor backfired in the initial version. She still has to review the new phrasing, but finds that students are not as sensitive as they were with the negative language.)

Maja's students like having the rubric, which captures the essence of what Maja expects from them, and they appreciate having time to experience what it means. Maja asks students to "allow themselves to fail," because her goal is to create a safe environment. She knows that her students can't learn unless they feel comfortable. By helping them with the rubric, she creates more symmetry between herself and her students compared to the asymmetrical, traditional teacher role. As a teacher, she is very much an observer, a key teacher position assumed by responsive teachers seeking to create an affirming environment. She uses wording like "our mantra" to develop a sense of shared community. Maja's visual for her role in relation to student facilitators shows how students are meant to interact with one another, not just with her (see the graphic in the rubric).

In these ways, Maja describes and models the interactive language structures of the social and academic behaviors she expects of her students. This explicit sharing of effective discourses helps to create an academic community of practice for the English language arts that prioritizes students' active involvement and ability to contribute to that community.

(See Chapter 6 for more details about Maja's assessment approaches.)

Reflective Student Self-Assessment/Whole Class Participation Rubric for Practicing YOUR VOICE

OUR MANTRA – to be used only with textual evidence

CONNECT TO ...

1. other parts of the passage
2. other parts of the novel/memoir/text as a whole
3. other forms of art (literature, movies), disciplines (human geography, biology, computer science...)
4. the real world or life
5. Essential Intellectual Traits (in other students and yourself – Seniors Only)

ALSO:

5. Piggyback on what other students have said.
6. Push back gently on what other students have said.
7. Use analytical verbs after summarizing to dig deeper.
8. Point out non sequiturs respectfully.

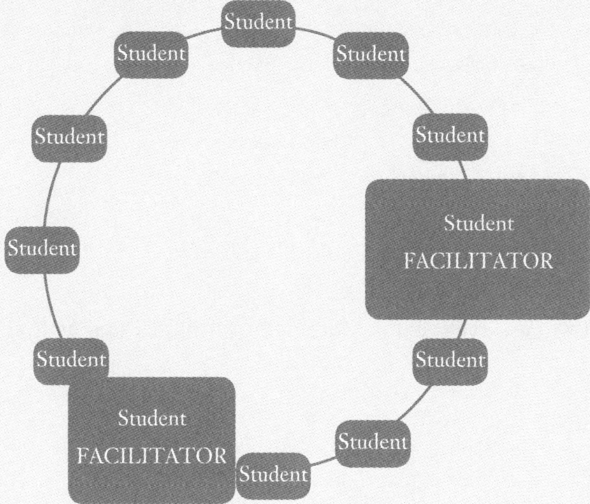

continued on next page

A = 90–100 Mastery = Distinguished Student Performance means that the student consistently . . .
- hits all of the above criteria genuinely (without just getting them out of the way) each month
- S.O.L.A.R.—participates and is engaged (e.g., never puts his/her head down but is awake and interested)
- embraces the idea of failure as an inevitable component of learning and success
- asks intellectually curious questions of her/himself, other students, teacher
- self-starts and offers to engage her/himself and others in place of the teacher when appropriate
- is consistently focused (no distractions causing discipline issues)
- doesn't complain but makes insightful suggestions [see note above about wording changes]
- engages other students and reminds them to stay on task
- does not dominate [now reads "monitors air time"]
- accurately justifies answers; explains assumptions, inferences, and reasoning; supports claims with evidence; draws justifiable conclusions; and accurately interprets textual material
- demonstrates improvement
- uses academic vocabulary and key concepts central to the course
- brings class materials (novel, notebook, journal . . .)

B = 80–89 Emerging Mastery = Proficient Student Performance means that the student . . .
- consistently hits 5–7 of the above criteria each month
- consistently participates and is engaged (e.g., never puts his/her head down but is awake and interested)
- usually embraces the idea of failure as an inevitable component of learning and success
- usually questions her/himself, other students, teacher
- usually self-starts and contributes to conversations in place of the teacher when appropriate
- is focused (no distractions causing discipline issues)
- doesn't complain but makes insightful suggestions
- usually engages other students and reminds them to stay on task
- may dominate class discussion (thus showing a lack of awareness of others)
- usually justifies answers; explains assumptions, inferences, and reasoning; supports claims with evidence; draws justifiable conclusions; and accurately interprets textual material
- demonstrates improvement with some lapses
- uses academic vocabulary and key concepts central to the course
- brings class materials (novel, notebook, journal . . .)

C = 70–79 Average = Below Mastery = Basic Student Performance means that the student . . .
- consistently hits 3 of the above criteria each month
- sometimes participates and is engaged
- more often than not embraces the idea of failure as an inevitable component of learning and success
- sometimes questions her/himself, other students, teacher
- sometimes self-starts and contributes to conversations in place of the teacher when appropriate
- is focused most of the time (few distractions causing discipline issues)
- usually doesn't complain but tries to make insightful suggestions

- sometimes engages other students and reminds them to stay on task
- sometimes may dominate class discussion (thus showing a lack of awareness of others) OR sometimes withdraws from class discussion
- sometimes justifies answers, explains assumptions, inferences, and reasoning; at times, supports claims with evidence, draws conclusions, interprets textual material
- demonstrates inconsistent improvement
- sometimes uses academic vocabulary and key concepts central to the course

D = 60–69 Below Average = Insufficient Student Performance means that the student . . .

- inconsistently hits 1–2 of the above criteria each month
- rarely participates and is engaged
- struggles with the idea of failure
- relies primarily on the teacher to provide motivation or participates in disengaging activities irrelevant to class outcomes
- relies on the teacher to be called on
- justifies few answers; seldom explains assumptions, inferences, and reasoning; provides ineffective support for claims; may draw unjustifiable conclusions; and may misinterpret textual material more often than not
- withdraws from class discussion and/or needs to be redirected and reminded to stay on task
- does not demonstrate significant improvement
- rarely uses academic vocabulary and key concepts central to the course

F = 0-59 Unsatisfactory Student Performance means that the student . . .

- withdraws from class discussion or engages in disengaging and distracting activities irrelevant to class outcomes each month
- demonstrates undisciplined or nonevident thinking
- entirely relies on the teacher in order to focus on the discussion
- doesn't justify answers, explain assumptions, inferences, or reasoning, support claims with evidence, draw justifiable conclusions, and/or accurately interpret textual material
- demonstrates little improvement
- does not demonstrate an understanding of key concepts central to the course

Structuring Active Interactions: Teacher Moves to Promote ELL Students' Active Engagement

Promoting Active Engagement

Echevarría, Vogt, and Short (2008), who have focused on how to make content comprehensible for language learners, describe ways that active engagement motivates students. Active engagement can mean anything that moves beyond a passive model of teacher-led instruction with no student involvement; when students are actively engaged, they are jointly working to learn. As you know, active engagement can provide more processing time than direct instruction does.

As you move toward active engagement, however, you may need to think carefully about the kinds of activities you sponsor and how those activities impact ELL students. Question-and-answer sessions during direct instruction, for example, can trigger anxieties, so structuring smaller groups instead can ease processing. In addition, using pairs, teams, or student facilitators can raise students' attention levels. For example, when students participate as discussion facilitators, they are actively engaged with the material.

Maja asks her students to take a turn facilitating a whole-class discussion, and she makes sure they are prepared to take on roles in discussion by preparing them with the discourses and structures they need to lead a class discussion.

Maja's Tips Handout for Student-Led Discussions

Tips for Conducting a Vibrant Whole-Class Facilitation by Students + (review rubric)

1. Meet with me a few days before your presentation if you need help with your questions.
2. Select one passage of no more than 20 lines, ideally between 5–15, photocopy or type it, annotate it thoroughly, and submit a copy to me right after your presentation. Don't forget to write your central question at the top.
3. Display your essential/central question at all times—on the board—and keep referring students back to it (1) before your presentation, (2) after ALL level 1 questions have been answered, and (3) after EACH level 2 question has been answered.
4. Display your annotated passage and keep your finger on the textual evidence you're referencing. Do not do a PPT with questions. In other words, have students look at the passage you are analyzing and not a PPT with questions.
5. Don't ask students to read your passage—you are the expert who's looked up all the new words, so YOU should read. And please, DO look up ALL new words, expressions, or allusions in your selected passage. Don't allow yourself to trip over any words or mispronounce them, because such faux pas undermine your credibility as a serious student.
6. Before asking any level 1 questions, help students establish the context. Ask them, "Who is talking to whom here? How do you know? Where is this scene in the book? What happened right before and right after?"

7. Regarding level 1 questions, ask the students: (1) Who is talking to whom? How do you know? (2) What is the setting? How do you know? (3) Ask about all pronouns and their antecedents, "Who is 'she'? What does 'it' refer to? What does 'which' refer to? How do you know?"
8. Constantly ask students to refer back to the text. Do NOT let them make assumptions.
9. Before moving on to the next question level, summarize the discussion so far and acknowledge a few students' contributions.
10. Explicitly state to the students when you're shifting from a level 1 to a level 2 or 3 question.
11. Remember, you are to have (1) 8–10 level 1 questions, (2) 1–2 level 2 questions, and (3) only 1 level 3 question. You will spend most time on level 2 questions.
12. Don't allow more than 5 minutes overall for your level 3 question—students can discuss the question with their elbow partner for 2 minutes, and then they can have 3 minutes to share.
13. When a student uses a "dead word," ask them to clarify, "What do you mean by 'thing'? Who is 'everybody'?"
14. If you are running out of time, DO NOT RUSH THROUGH YOUR QUESTIONS! If students are digging deeper and deeper and referencing the text, let them enjoy their discussion and cut out the rest of your questions. You are under NO obligation to ask all of your questions; rather, for an A or a B, pay attention to the DEPTH (quality) of discussion, not the BREADTH (coverage, quantity) of discussion.
15. Get EVERYBODY involved for an A by having each student talk to an elbow partner.
16. Time the students and tell them, "You'll have 2 minutes to discuss how Larry's mental and emotional journey relates to what we just said."
17. Have students move around, shift, raise hands because students love movement.
18. Comment on EVERY student's comment in order to acknowledge every participating student.
19. When you compliment students, be specific: "I love that you made the connection between the long description of Larry's eyes and his hands." Never say, "Good job." Students love compliments and will want to participate more if given positive feedback.
20. If a discussion is going off on a tangent, quickly summarize and redirect: "Clearly, we are feeling passionate about the subject, and I thank you for that, but if we could go back to our central question, that'd be great."
21. End your presentation by thanking the class. Do NOT say, "That's it. We're done."

Structuring Ways to Respond and Elaborate

Promoting effective student discussion is key, especially in classrooms with ELL students, and making expectations explicit is also important, as noted in Maja's example. This means offering support through written and oral models of effective responses and questions. Note how Maja's tips offer explicit wording for what to say and not say, similar to the kinds of moves she models in class as the teacher facilitator.

For example, Maja and other teachers with experience working with ELLs know that effective teachers encourage ELL students to elaborate and not just give a "yes," "no," or other one-word response. This means giving students time to express themselves and resisting our natural inclination to complete their sentences.

You can ask, "What else?" or other questions to help students elaborate. Patiently employing wait-time can help ELL students engage in the discussion. Giving them options to "phone a friend" or consult written work also can help. For instance, letting students "phone a friend" (e.g., allowing them to ask a colleague for help on a response) can help students understand the value of collaboration and that they are not perceived as somehow "lesser" when they ask someone else for help. Written responses, to substitute for or expand on a response in a whole-class discussion, encourage students to elaborate and provide the needed challenge that many ELL students desire.

In Practice: Teacher Moves That Encourage ELL Students' Contributions

Key Practices in This Vignette

- Providing multiple participation options (e.g., written, oral)
- Varying group sizes and structures (e.g., Think-Pair-Share)
- Defining and modeling effective (verbal/nonverbal) participation
- Teaching both listening and speaking skills

As part of acceptable class participation, Maja provides the option to write and/or to work in smaller groups as a way to support students' ability to elaborate. In a whole-class discussion, she will sometimes pause the action to encourage participation by different students or to encourage different types of participation.

Maja tells the class, "Not everyone here is ready to speak to thirty others." So she asks students to Think-Pair-Share: First, she asks them to "think" and jot notes. They can then participate verbally in pairs, read from their notes during the pair sharing, and turn in their notes after the whole-class discussion.

Maja adapts the way she structures participation based on her observations of students. One student recently arrived from Vietnam[2] seemed self-conscious about speaking and was initially quiet in discussions. To better help this young woman, Maja watched her body language in the whole-class discussion, noting that the student only raised a hand to respond with a short recall answer so that she wouldn't need to speak much or have her accent heard. And yet the student's writing was amazing. These observations prompted Maja to tell students they could participate verbally or turn in their notes after whole-class discussions. Given this kind of flexibility, over time the student gained the confidence to participate verbally in more complex ways.

Another student seemed self-conscious when speaking, and other students sometimes struggled to understand what he was saying, but Maja noticed that he had a great sense of humor and so built on this strength during one-on-one, small-group, and written responses. Over time he became one of the best classroom facilitators, using the methods Maja offered for effective participation. She also notices that sometimes extremely sharp students have even more anxiety about participating if they are concerned about how their language use may be perceived, so she models how to focus on the depth of what someone is saying in their responses. This modeling makes expectations explicit for both the student speakers and the student listeners.

For example, in a discussion about the author's description of a key character's erratic actions in *The Color of Water*, a student says, "Ruth looking schizo [schizophrenic], it gets more conflict."

Maja says, "Okay, so what is the 'conflict' we're seeing from 'Ruth looking schizo'?"

In this way, Maja picks up a key part of what is being said and directly quotes the student (rather than verbally correcting the word choice) as she helps the class continue the discussion based on the depth of the comment.

Using Responsive Interaction Structures That Promote Varied Language Uses

Research shows that ELL students have more opportunities to learn and use language when given a variety of interaction structures (Ariza, 2010; Vásquez, Hansen, & Smith, 2013; Vogt, Echevarría, & Short, 2010). Here are some types you are likely already familiar with:

- pairs
- small groups
- literature circles
- Think-Pair-Share
- jigsaw
- debates
- dialogue journals
- dinner party

2. Students' details may be adjusted to mask identity.

- phone a friend
- technology-mediated interactions

Part of the reason for implementing these different configurations is to provide multiple and varied opportunities for using language, including oral, written, academic, and/or interpersonal language. Maja describes the ways changing structures can help students "share their thinking and receive input from all of their peers, which is a great community-building tool." What we see in her classroom in the earlier descriptions are the multiple ways she builds the activities and opportunities for response. Overall, Maja's classroom employs four main structures that enable her to provide these opportunities, and her students consistently work in pairs and small groups in addition to independent and whole-class work:

1. Independent work: You might see her students engaging in quickwrites, annotating texts, or reading.
2. Pair work: Students exchange viewpoints, listen, read together, and/or write. They sometimes turn to their "elbow partner." Alternatively, the students and Maja assign pairs (or groups) together.
3. Small-group work: Students often work in groups of four. Maja describes how group work (and varied grouping choices) can provide bonding experiences during which students are given options so they feel invested and empowered.
4. Whole-class discussion: These discussions are sometimes teacher-led and sometimes student-led.

Most good teachers include a variety of participation structures. We need to ask ourselves critical questions about our ELL students in order to include and vary these participation structures to ensure that the classroom setup is responsive to their varied needs. We know that it's especially crucial for ELL students to have genuine opportunities to use language during authentic content area activities, and the ways we structure these are going to vary based on our mix of students. A student like Luis, who is in a silent stage, will need support that is different from that of a student like Diana, who feels most comfortable communicating orally, depending on whether the structure prioritizes oral or written language abilities. Luis may need help from a classmate who speaks his language, or he may be able to use visuals or acting to participate. (For an excellent, comprehensive resource for considering a specific student's stage of language acquisition and which strategies might support that particular stage, see www.colorincolorado.org/article/language-acquisition-overview.)

Because of differences like these, ongoing student feedback is a key component of how Maja groups students: "In fact, the more I ask for my students' feedback on rubrics, activities, seating arrangement, and the more input they have, the more involved they are." Although this kind of input is important in any classroom, it's especially important in a classroom with ELLs. Thus, Maja lets students shape her practice, which reflects her understanding that one-size-fits-all instruction does *not* fit all. This kind of student feedback takes on heightened importance with multilingual learners because it helps students see themselves as active participants who are setting goals related to language learning. It also keeps us from making assumptions based on superficial understandings of complex intersections of adolescents' social, linguistic, and academic development. Of course, teachers like Maja also use their observations to shape how they establish effective grouping, ensuring a wide range of collaborative options.

Also based on her observations and student feedback, Maja considers the sequencing for types of groups or pair work. Independent work often functions as a first step. Once students have notes and page numbers from the text to help them share textual evidence, Maja holds them accountable. In terms of independent work, Maja notes that her ELL students may see independent writing as a refuge, a way to collect their thoughts. She uses independent writing in preparation for collaborative work as a way to push her students, especially dominant discussers who may be native speakers, to give examples. This gives all students a chance to get inside the discussion.

In pair work, Maja sees a chance for some ELL students to take first steps outside of themselves. To structure the paired interactions, she models how to be respectful, how to listen to evidence that others provide, and how to create positive feelings in the interaction. She finds that for ELLs, sharing with one other person may lead them to be less anxious about performing than they would be in a larger group, at least initially. She notices that students are often more open in pairs and are less guarded than they are in bigger groups.

Pair work is sometimes used as a warm-up to working with larger groups. Because Maja has noticed that some ELL students hide in small groups of three to four peers, she seeks to interrupt this pattern by giving clear participation structures for small groups. For example, she asks, "Have one person speak for the next two minutes with the other students listening and taking notes." And then she has the other students take their turns in the role of vocal participant.

Maja also circulates during group and pair work. She may notice a student who is blushing and give that student a break from speaking. She asks students to share specific page numbers and read a quotation, modeling how to be immersed in the content while reading and responding to a text.

In her prompting, Maja is careful not to recast what ELL students say in front of other students. Instead, she models how small groups can provide a safe space for students to trip over their words and get lost as they try to make meaning.

Maja calls her approach "honoring the struggle" of language learning. When we encounter visitors from another country who struggle to speak English, our impulse is often to rephrase what they are saying in English. However, Maja remembers from her own experience how that struggle was a key part of her language learning. When we cut off or recast what students are saying (usually out of compassion), we may not be supporting them the way we think we are. Instead, ELLs may interpret our actions as a lack of interest in waiting to listen and make meaning of what they are saying, or that we find the speaker flawed and in need of correction.

"Let them make their meaning," Maja says, which can take patience. She considers this quality so important for herself and for her students that she highlights *listening and patience* in her classroom rubric.

In Practice: Grouping Based on Understandings of ELL Students' Needs

Key Practices in This Vignette

- Thinking out loud
- Rephrasing during modeling
- Using silence and gestures

So how does Maja use understanding of language to make sure that grouping is responsive to ELLs? When Maja taught ESL classes, she considered both ability level and language background in her grouping. She sometimes grouped students linguistically to provide comfort and the ability to target skills in a particular language. She also varied groups in the beginning based on ethnic diversity to help students move out of initial social insecurities.

Now, in her more heterogeneous classrooms of multilingual students, where many are Generation 1.5, she sometimes uses more random methods for grouping (like counting off counterclockwise or naming how spicy they like their food), especially later in the year as students become more comfortable. These more random methods help students get to know how other students think.

With ELL students, Maja considers in particular the time of year and how comfortable specific students are with oral participation and collaborative work. For example, one young man who was often quiet in class seemed to hide in the back by the window. In the beginning of the year, Maja provided opportunities for him to choose his own group with other young men with whom he seemed more comfortable. Over time she observed him gaining confidence and gravitating even more toward that group. As the group continued to work together, Maja noticed that she could hear his voice more often and that his voice was louder as the group collaborated, a sign that he was becoming more confident and perhaps ready for whole-group and new-group sharing. Her observations of his interpersonal connections helped her determine when he would be ready for grouping with less familiar students.

In both small-group and large-group discussions, Maja models thinking out loud in an academic conversation and using academic vocabulary. She often talks, stops, goes back, and rephrases: "What am I noticing here about what's happening between these characters? Aha! That's an unexpected twist! Let's see, what do you call that "'unexpected twist'"? Ummm . . . irony!"

Maja also notes that silence can be important in a discussion. For instance, when her ninth graders get stuck in a coverage mindset, where they have a lot of ideas and move too quickly from one topic to another, she asks them to "slow down." Sometimes they need to stop and record what they are noticing as they analyze the text, a skill she works to improve for all her students, but particularly for those like Diana, who feels much more comfortable communicating in oral English.

In one such situation, Maja holds up her hand in the whole-group discussion and presses it into the air like a stop sign. She asks students to stop talking with her: "This is a moment to slow down. Why don't we write about this now? We've been talking about this for the last twenty minutes. Now it's time to slow down and write about what we're thinking." She models how to pause with her pen in the air and alternately think, write, and look at the annotated text.

Tips for Responsive Grouping of Students: Consider Language and Learning Objectives

Most teachers and scholars agree with Maja that it's not useful to put all ELL students in the same group on a regular basis. Instead, just as you would in any ELA class, consider your goals and objectives in relation to how partners are chosen or how to group students. But when working with ELLs, add to those goals and objectives the underlying language understandings necessary for language learners to be successful in groups:

- What writing, speaking, and other language use skills (i.e., language demands–both academic and social) are required in the lesson?
- What are the interactional goals?
- How do language demands intersect with these goals and your lesson objectives?
- What are the lesson's objectives? How are they linked to how students are grouped (homogeneous versus heterogeneous)?

Supporting the Range of Voices in Your Class

Many ELL students experience a silent period when learning language, as demonstrated by Luis in the opening portraits and in the following vignette. Students may be silenced due to social concerns or even cultural expectations. How should we interpret student silence in a multilingual classroom?

Linguists have identified various levels of speech emergence (see Table 3.1). In some stages, vocabulary may be more receptive (e.g., see Krashen & Terrell, 1983) and ELL students may be limited to short phrases with a smaller vocabulary of a few hundred words. These students may be able to follow a command, respond to yes or no questions, or respond with a combination of gestures, movement, and visuals. They may look down in our classes or avoid participation.

Table 3.1. Description of One Model for Speech Emergence in Language Acquisition
Note: Linguists offer multiple models for language acquisition and possible stages. Table 3.1 summarizes one way of thinking about key stages for second language acquisition based on work by Krashen and Terrell (1983) and examples from ELA teachers.

Description of Speech Emergence in Language Acquisition (based on Krashen and Terrell, 1983)

Stages of Speech Emergence	What Does It Look/Sound Like for a Student Learning English?	Some Pedagogical Implications for ELA Teachers
Preproduction	A student may · be silent · repeat exactly what you say (parroting) · have access to only 500 (or less) English words	Consider that · students may listen more than they speak · students may face challenges due to smaller vocabulary · visuals or gestures may help
Early Production	A student may · start to develop more vocabulary (have access to 1000+ words in English)	Consider · supports and scaffolds to help students access ELA content and vocabulary · allowing short responses
Speech Emergence	A student may · initiate peer conversations · use simple phrases · have access to 3,000+ words in English · not understand yet when you are joking	Consider how · grammar or punctuation errors may become apparent as more structures are learned and actually used · a dialogue journal can support your ELA communication
Intermediate Fluency	A student may · have access to 6,000+ English words; usually takes at least 3–5 years · sometimes use complex syntax in writing and/or speaking	Consider that · a student will have more ability to answer in longer responses · development may vary in different aspects of acquisition based on experiences in other languages
Advanced Fluency	A student · may reach this stage in 5–7 years · is usually not in ESL classes anymore · may sound like a "native" speaker	Consider that · it may take up to 10 years to reach this stage with academic language · students will need your support with different ELA language demands (e.g., types of writing or other language tasks)

Reflecting on this silent period, especially as ELL students integrate into mainstream classrooms, Maja notes, "This is expected. They are just processing; we need to honor that." She supports this period by not putting silent or uncomfortable students on the spot, allowing opportunities for writing, and easing students into the increasing levels of participation in small groups. As described in more detail in the vignette, modeling responses can help students learn ways to start participating in small groups, such as focusing on textual evidence rather than on their own accents. She also taps into students' excitement about and connections with a text to encourage participation.

In Practice: Supporting and Affirming ELL Students in Small Groups

Key Practices in This Vignette

- Not recasting a student's response
- Monitoring groups and modeling responses (e.g., use of textual evidence)
- Providing opportunities to respond in writing and at varied rates
- Showing appreciation for students' strengths in group work

Maja notices how softly a new student is speaking in class. She also hears the other students' silence after the new student first speaks. Maja knows it's important not to recast what the student has said, because she wants to send the message that the focus in this class is not on speaking in perfect, unaccented English.

Similarly, Maja monitors her small groups. She might notice a student with an accent who is looking down, avoiding eye contact, and trying to be invisible. When she sees this kind of withdrawal, her response is to listen in on that group's conversation. She circulates over to the small group and listens carefully.

In these situations, Maja chooses to model how to respond to the most salient word or phrase in the *idea* the student has raised. Her goal is to convey understanding of what the student said and repeat it verbatim—not recast it into her own words.

She responds to the content of what an ELL student is saying. If the student says, "Ruth McBride looked crazy while riding her bike," Maja picks the most charged word to push students toward an evocative response.

"Yes! She looked CRAZY! Where in the text can your group find an example?" and Maja prompts students to share specific textual examples aloud. This helps all students because students who are confident in the oral discussion may not always go back to the text to support their responses. She also models how students can read an example directly from the book to make sure they know that sharing a direct, textual example is fair game in the discussion as part of illustrating a point. Many of her ELL students are "all about the text," and she can highlight this as a strength that supports their peers' learning.

Learning about Students: Provide Varied Oral and Written Opportunities for Students to Share with You

A variety of oral and written interactions with students can help you learn more about your ELL students. In some of the chapter-opening portraits, for example, the students' teachers could have built more responsive classroom spaces by taking the time to truly learn about their multilingual students. Knowing that we have ELL students in our mainstream classrooms means that our perspectives about how race and language intersect may need to be stretched, as Áron's teacher's response from the opening portraits demonstrates. Some teachers may assume that if students appear "white" and sound like native speakers, they are monolingual, an assumption grounded in myths about language that can sometimes intersect with beliefs about race. As with many Generation 1.5 students, language learners and multilingual students are not always easily identifiable—race and accents can blind us to their language knowledge. Maja warns, often students "don't have an accent: we just have to stop being superficial about listening to our students."

We also need to learn about students' language use (and beliefs about that use), both before and during family interactions. You might discover that some families buy into the myth that parents should speak only English at home, even though research shows that this strategy can actually strain parent-child bonds, has not been demonstrated to increase English proficiency, and can actually cause more harm (e.g., through subtractive bilingualism) for young children who do not gain access to the nuances of their parents' native language. Students also may have internalized beliefs about their proficiencies as readers, speakers, or writers in English and/or additional languages. Even at the college level, I encounter many students who believe that speaking in a language, like Spanish, prior to English has had a negative influence on their writing abilities, even when there is little evidence to support this belief. Yet when asked, the same students are often proud that they dream in a language other than English or can communicate with family members in another language.

So how do we learn more about these various beliefs and elements of students' identities and language use? First, make sure you are learning about students in multiple ways. Maja offers a good model of how a teacher can learn about students in various ways in order to create a more responsive classroom environment.

> 1. First, Maja learns about students through *varied curricular structures:*
>
> "I learn a great deal about my students through one-on-one conferences, small-group discussions, grade defenses [Reflective Self-Assessments], and email correspondence."
>
> These varied structures give us a chance to notice what students are able to do in writing and reading, not just what they are unable to do. In

turn, this helps us acknowledge interpersonal and language strengths and thus position ELL students positively so that they know what they can contribute.

2. Second, she learns about them through *brief interpersonal exchanges:*

"What is that book you're reading?" and "I love your new haircut."

3. Third, she identifies a lot about their abilities and lives through *their writing:*

"As for their abilities specifically, I like to look at their writing: are they ELL or Gen 1.5, are they able to code-switch, do they have a disability, are they "'task completionists'" or "'deep thinkers,'" what their home life is like, what is their sexual orientation and are they struggling with it, do they have a sense of humor, what makes them tick. In writing, students will reveal incredible facts, secrets, and troubles because when they write, they don't need to perform in front of their peers. They can be immersed in their own world and ask for help."

All of these ways provide different opportunities for students to share their interests and abilities; in particular, you can use these different types of interactions to learn more about students' understandings of language and culture.

First Steps to Applying Language Understandings to Create a Responsive Classroom

We need to understand ourselves, our language understandings, and ELL students' strengths and abilities in order to create a responsive space for rigorous learning. Really knowing the range of our students may take time and even involve researching our own practice to learn more about the students in our classrooms (Boyd et al., 2006), a topic I discuss more in Chapter 6. However, as part of developing a responsive classroom community, here are some initial steps to better understanding ELL students.

Step 1: Avoid Panic Mode

For a new teacher or new teacher of a language learner, it might be tempting to panic or to wallow in denial about having ELL students in the mainstream classroom. Sometimes schools do segregate students (e.g., newcomers like Luis) by putting them in a small group outside of the mainstream classroom. While in certain situations this is helpful to students, often this separation actually stymies students' academic growth (Goldenberg & Coleman, 2010) and prevents students like Luis, Vanessa, Áron, and others from experiencing the rigorous learning they need. Not all schools have the resources for a separate class. If you teach in a district with a lower number of ELL students, they may be placed directly into an ELA classroom. In other larger districts, there may be a dedicated ESL staff; ELA teachers may not see ELL students until they are "FLEPed" (considered to fit the category of "Former Limited English Proficient") into mainstream classrooms after demonstrating some level of proficiency in English speaking, writing, listening, and reading, usually on a standardized test.

Given this range, investigate your situation for its possibilities. Here are some questions you might ask:

- Do some students need (or have) an initial pullout experience? Is it appropriate for me to have a student who is new to the United States in my class?
- What terminology is being used for my students by the district, my school, the state, and/or the students? Is this terminology negative, limiting, or affirming? What do I understand this terminology to mean? Who can I ask in order to learn more?
- How comfortable are my students and I with encountering some discomfort—e.g., across language "barriers" or cultures—while communicating with others?

The last question refers to what research tells us is a need to be open to discomfort in multilingual or multicultural interactions (Case, 2015). Reframing our own initial panic reactions can help us support our non-ELL (and ELL) students' reactions to difference. Communication across languages requires two-way understanding and a willingness to be open to listening to others. In fact, metaphors other than "overcoming language barriers" can be more useful in considering these situations. Students learn to close gaps between each other by "opening spaces," such as using techniques beyond words to communicate and not giving up when oral communication is not possible or easy in one language (Case, 2015). This stance involves accepting discomfort as a potential part of the exchange and entails a desire to be proactive in approaching and engaging others. For instance, Luis's silent stage may require peers and teachers who are actively trying to communicate, knowing that communication may not be quick or easy and may require close observation and innovation.

Step 2: Avoid Confusing Difference with Deficiency

Even though we know that ELL students who struggle in English may be gifted learners in their own language, it's sometimes hard to remember that when we're in the throes of a busy classroom. Assessing each student and situation is critical. Of course, pretty much no one learns from extremes of grammar instruction, so parking a newcomer like Luis in the corner alone with English grammar worksheets because we're not sure what else to do is a surefire way to kill motivation.

According to Johnson (2008), some of the brightest students may actually struggle more with language learning due to a low tolerance for ambiguity. All types of language learning (speaking, listening, reading, writing) can pose challenges for different students, as Ortmeier-Hooper (2013a) and others have noted; some students will have strengths in some areas but not others: e.g., they may speak easily in their second language but have trouble reading; they may read well but have trouble writing.

As you may have experienced yourself, language learning is a long, ongoing, and complicated process. There's a reason why it typically takes three generations for immigrants to acquire fluency in a new language. One misconception is that recent immigrants are learning English at slower rates than past generations. This simply isn't true (Johnson, 2008). In fact, as schools and classrooms provide language acquisition services, we are supporting a new generation that will likely not be forced to live in language enclaves as in past generations. What may be trickiest in many school systems is to truly support a bilingual student like valedictorian Vanessa by encouraging biliteracy or multiliteracy.

The pervasive myths about second language acquisition mean that responsive teachers of ELL students need to advocate for their students by helping to "dispel the myth that ELLs are not learning English quickly enough" (Johnson, 2008, p. 60). It can take more than ten years to reach the proficiency in English to do grade-level work.

Step 3: Consider the Implications for the Labels Being Used

Label distinctions matter. Identities can differ greatly when a student identifies as a refugee as opposed to a voluntary migrant or immigrant (Ortmeier-Hooper, 2013b). A student who has arrived in the United States voluntarily is much more likely to be motivated to learn about the language and culture of his or her new country than a refugee student like David (another student you'll recall from the opening portraits), who may either have less opportunity to maintain positive contact with his country of origin or may have less desire to assimilate quickly (see Ogbu & Simons, 1998). Understanding this distinction can help us notice and respond to the desire of someone like David to separate himself from peers.

These differences provide a wonderful opportunity to support critical thinking and pedagogy. Creating a safe environment in which students can explore, share, and understand multiple cultural and linguistic perspectives (though not forcing them when they aren't comfortable disclosing personal information) encourages all students to expand their thinking. Students can explore a range of cultures in class through the topics discussed, authors read, and literature included. For instance, students might connect or contrast their personal experiences during discussions of literature and literary themes, such as how class is defined in a cross-cultural text like *Persepolis*, offering opportunities to build on students' individual experiences. However, students who have experienced displacement due to refugee status may be grappling with ambivalent emotions related to their country of origin.

The key is to provide an opportunity or invitation to share, not impose a mandate. We can do so through multiple entry points. Maja, for example, asks students to delve deeper into various cultural perspectives in their readings by inviting them to make connections, as in "What do we do in our cultural contexts? In my culture . . ." Culture is an anchor that enables students to draw on multiple perspectives in addition to their own. Some students who see characters in *Persepolis* as more rooted in "their culture" might decide to "become experts" by sharing their perspectives. Maja asks both her multilingual and native English speakers to translate their own cultural experiences in relation to the cultural experiences they read about. Her goal for her multilingual students: "don't make them feel foreign" with her curricular choices (either spotlighted or ignored). Having students study a variety of texts such as *Things Fall Apart*, *The Color of Water*, and *Othello* lets students be "alternatively at home and also read satellite texts," according to Maja.

Another important issue is how your students label and perceive different types of English. Have they already learned English in an international context? They may, for example, already use a different variety of English, like Nigerian English, that has different lexical or syntactical structures. Dellicarpini (2009) reminds us that differences in American, British, and Indian Englishes affect understanding, such as *dress* to refer to men's, women's, and children's clothing in Indian English, or *banger* to mean sausage in British English. Depending on how you notice and respond, differences can lead to an exchange that calls on students' knowledge, leads to teasing by others, or results in student resistance. Therefore, it's important to note that World Englishes, perceptions of American English, and language learning in other languages are linked to past school experiences and shape what students believe counts as language.

Perhaps even more important, myths about which languages or accents are better or superior can lead students to hide or stigmatize their language use (Johnson, 2008). Maja has observed that, in her past ESL classes, with students from up to twenty-five different countries, different groups have sometimes made fun of others. When, for example, some ESL students made fun of others from Latinx or African backgrounds, Maja took advantage of the negative moment to start conversations about perspective taking and understanding other people's emotions, and she drew on her own multilingual experiences to talk about the effect of language and culture bashing on one's confidence and sense of community. Incidentally, their conversations about these themes led to students learning a lot of English.

These critical perspectives on language can be important for all students, especially since some scholars have argued that language discrimination functions as a backdoor to racism or classism (see Lippi-Green, 2012).

Step 4: Develop Your Empathy with Language Learning

> "Never make fun of someone who speaks broken English. It means they know another language." —H. Jackson Brown Jr.

Language is an inherently personal part of our identities. If you are like me and many Americans, you don't speak a second language fluently; your foreign language instruction probably began (and perhaps ended) at the secondary level. As Brown (2007) reminds us, it is hypocritical for the majority of Americans to be impatient with ELLs who they feel aren't learning language fast enough when we have barely delved into a second language ourselves. As mentioned earlier and discussed in more detail in Table 3.1 (p. 56), it's estimated that advanced fluency in a language can take up to a decade to achieve, and this is the level of fluency often needed for content area learning. (See colorincolorado.org for "Stages of Language Acquisition," an overview that provides in-depth criteria for assessing your students' stages and considering your possible responses.)

My attempts to become more fluent in an additional language sensitized me to the challenges facing many of our students, though I also recognize the limits of my experiences. As I studied Spanish throughout secondary school and higher education, I felt the tensions of being a language learner who could read proficiently enough to pass a graduate-level translation exam but still felt too tongue-tied to use my limited oral Spanish with native speakers. Despite many years of study, my reading and writing skills remain quite different from my oral language skills based on the contexts of my language use. And the contexts of language use matter: while I was able to translate the academic language used in literary theory and literary texts, it was unlikely that I could have accurately translated a colloquial conversation.

Experienced teachers develop their responsiveness through empathy. Ruth, a veteran ELA high school teacher, describes her response based on her language learning:

> I have just awe in front of my students who have had to learn English as school-aged students. I also can tell from a mile away which of my students are not native speakers in their homes, even if they were born here, because of their use of prepositions. And I have such empathy; I mean how do you know which preposition to use in English? And I remember the same dilemma in learning French: is it "a la" or "en" when you say, "I'm going to America"? My heart goes out to them and I have a lot of patience with them as a result.

Similarly, Maja describes her empathy with Generation 1.5 students:

> I'm aware of their struggles. . . . I've been there. I know exactly what their problems are . . . it was something recently. There was a student misusing some word and I almost remembered from my own experience having misused that word.

The reality is that many of us either haven't had these language learning experiences or we need to remind ourselves of these experiences. It's also important that we model for our students a key understanding: language learning is a long and complicated process. The process of learning a new language is not linear or applied evenly across contexts, language types, and demands.

In Practice: Meghan's Experience Thinking about Language Learning

Key Practices in This Vignette

- Using multiple languages and technology to differentiate and provide access to grade-level content
- Reflecting on our language learning experiences and assumptions
- Modeling openness to multiple perspectives and using research for new ideas

Meghan, a middle school student teacher, thought back to how hard she'd had to pay attention to instructions in her high school Spanish class, and how she often used the textbook CD to listen to the instructions again and again because she felt uncomfortable asking the teacher to repeat himself.

Now, as she works to make modifications in her middle school ELA class at a private school with limited services for newcomer students, Meghan recalls this experience and connects it to a recent article she read, "Success with ELLs" (DelliCarpini, 2009). When she can, she provides instructions in the students' home languages, like Spanish. However, to accommodate a newcomer student from Kenya, Meghan let him listen to prompts on his e-reader as many times as he needed so that he was getting immersed in English but at his own speed. Although Meghan circulates to check in with the students, they have a chance to access directions on their own until she can get to them.

Meghan has also started modeling for students how to treat newcomers as vital members of the class to help avoid having other students treat them as outsiders. She models referring to different aspects of her identity and demonstrating acceptance of others, such as how she expanded her understanding of the stereotypes she grew up with through a recent reading of a book, and why she is careful about making assumptions about others due to the hurtful perceptions her family faced as new immigrants to a rural area.

Step 5: Use Students' Language Knowledge in Class; Show Respect for Language Variation

As we inquire into our own language use and analyze the political stakes of using language, we can highlight that knowledge in class to emphasize the value of linguistic diversity.

Teacher Ruth describes ways she promotes the idea of linguistic diversity:

> I give them examples of [language use]—for example, in South Africa a lot of people speak three or four languages in one sentence. In Zurich you say, "Merci veil mal—" you use a French word and a German word together to say "Thank you very much," that language is just something that comes out of people. And we need to respect it. I know just enough about other languages to be dangerous, and so I am constantly saying to them, "Sure you know what some Latinate word means because look, there's the Spanish right in there." And so I'm always putting Spanish and French words on the board because some of [the students] are studying French.

Other teachers focus on the ways literature might showcase different dialects or languages and how authors use that difference as a way to express characterization. Even when teaching something that seems classically English, like Dickens's *A Christmas Carol*, you may learn that students need to grapple with the ways the English language is used very differently in literature that represents a different cultural and historical context. We can teach literature like *A Christmas Carol* (or a Shakespeare play or Chaucer's *Canterbury Tales*) to begin the discussion of how English varies over time and place.

Maja also interjects language knowledge into everyday discussions in her classroom and uses students' knowledge to explore word origins. For example, when students were analyzing a poem, the second to last stanza contained the word *Penultimate*, and she drew out what her Spanish speakers in the class knew—that it meant "second to last." In Spanish the word is *penúltimo* and shares Latin roots (*paeno* [almost] and *ultimus* [last]) with the English word. Her students are also familiar with *last* in Spanish, or *ultimo*. For Maja, this is an example of the "many connections that [teachers] can make with their students' backgrounds" to promote engagement.

Maja also encourages students to share their knowledge with one another. During a lesson on allusions, for instance, students read the sentence "New York is the mecca of fashion," and Maja's Muslim students talked about their understandings of Mecca as both a word and a place. Maja enjoys making connections with students' backgrounds because "they love it and get engaged."

In Practice: Reasons for Building on Students' Language Knowledge

Key Practices in This Vignette

- Using home language assets to increase content understanding for all
- Eliciting student participation and knowledge
- Asking questions about word origins

Whenever Maja introduces a new word, she questions her students about its morphology and etymology, especially encouraging students whose home language could add insight to the conversation. Maja describes the reasons she constantly looks for ways to incorporate students' language knowledge into her academic learning:

> Students in general enjoy discussing origins of words, especially the "big words" because such a discussion becomes a critical bonding moment especially since most "big words" are of Latin origin. For example, the Spanish speakers as well as the other speakers of Romance languages become excited by this opportunity to share their language knowledge.

Chapter 4 describes additional specific examples of how you can build on the word knowledge your students may bring to the classroom.

Creating Resonance in the Responsive Classroom: Who We Are and How It Affects the Environment

We know that the demographic of teachers has become increasingly white, monolingual, female, and middle class, and these teachers will teach an increasingly linguistically, culturally, and economically diverse group of students (Hollins & Torres Guzman, 2006; Melnick & Zeichner, 1998). I've experienced how many schools struggle with cultural and linguistic mismatches between student and teacher populations. And, yes, language-related misunderstandings have taken place in my English language arts classrooms as I worked with students who came from multiple cultural and linguistic backgrounds, just as described by many other teachers and researchers (Delpit, 1995; Fecho, 2004; Hyland, 2005).

This is exactly why it's important to think through who we are and how we can make our classrooms responsive. We know that if dissonance occurs, students might not disclose their language histories. But we also know that students bring to the classroom many facets of identity that can lead to silencing or lack of motivation if interclass relationships aren't addressed.

Teachers like Ruth, Maja, and others approach their engagement with students through a positive, affirmative stance. They foster affirming discourses that create a classroom community. To do so, they invite students to share their funds of knowledge, both personal information and personal stories (Ortmeier-Hooper, 2013a, 2013b). As they think strategically about language, however, teachers also need to avoid stigmatizing students based on such disclosures, such as making deficit assumptions based on language learning status, which could lead to limiting recommendations for honors and other promotions (e.g., Enright, 2013; Ortmeier-Hooper, 2013b). For instance, we have to be careful that we don't make deficit assumptions when we learn that a student is multilingual, or limit students' access to high-level coursework based on this disclosure. Instead, we need to help students realize the ways in which their multilingual language use could be a benefit in honors courses or critical thinking projects. Research (e.g., Ortmeier-Hooper, 2013b) reminds us that often ELL students avoid sharing their ELL affiliation, even when it means gaining access to school resources that might be available to help them. School demographics may affect your approach: How many ELL students are there? How are they perceived?

In the end, our interactions need to be balanced. Researcher Cummins (2000) states, "School success is created in educator-student interactions that simultaneously affirm student identities and provide a balance of explicit instruction focused on academic language, content, and strategies together with extensive opportunities for students to engage with literacy and collaborative critical inquiry" (p. 268). This balance comes from knowing who our students are and supporting their abilities to work together, understanding multiple facets of language, and showing our care for and appreciation of them. The possibilities for collaborative, critical inquiry expand as we diversify our classrooms and our understanding of who we all are in those classrooms.

Next Steps: Structuring Responsive Learning Spaces in ELA Classrooms

In this chapter, we discussed how, in the quest to shape a responsive classroom, we need to understand the role of discourse—how we talk about language, use language, and structure language learning interactions—in order to support ELL students.

Let's look at key aspects of understanding the interpersonal and language-related dynamics of relationships in the classroom. These areas help us to:

1. Consider our own experiences and their implications for relationships with ELL students

2. Contemplate the ways we welcome critical thinking and engage in critical pedagogy
3. Develop a dynamic approach to the learning environment

To provide respect and rigor in the ELA classroom, responsive teachers enact ways of knowing ELL students by taking time to learn about students' range of literacy histories and complex identities as learners and adolescents; positioning ELL students as valued members of the mainstream classroom through purposeful student-teacher interactions as well as peer-to-peer interactions; and supporting students' voices in the mainstream ELA classroom by offering various avenues of participation and recognizing students' strengths and abilities.

Getting Started: Questions to Ask Yourself about Shaping a Responsive Classroom Environment

Exploring What You Know about Your Students

Who are my students?

What do they know?

What are their expectations of me as a teacher?

How do they interact with other students?

How do they self-identify?

Are there distinctions between linguistic and cultural knowledge (e.g., Latinx students who aren't literate in Spanish)?

Creating Safe Classroom Discourse

Who is doing the talking in class?

Are students elaborating beyond yes/no answers?

Do students know what constitutes a successful response?

Do students have both oral and written opportunities for responding?

Chapter Four

Understanding Language as a Resource for Academic and Social Contexts

Maja notices that many of her Generation 1.5 students struggle to use writing as a means for exploring their thinking. They seem reluctant and unsure of themselves when asked to respond in writing. She wants to build ways for them to see writing as useful and as a way to make connections. She hears their reluctance to write early in the year in response to an independent brainstorming prompt based on The Color of Water. *Maja asks them to write an arguable statement in response to a scene in which James McBride describes his mother, Ruth, riding a rickety bicycle through Harlem, the only white woman on the street. A few students are stuck.*

"Can't we just talk about it?"

"If you just talk," Maja says, "You may forget about some of your ideas; they may slip your mind."

She sits down next to the students at a table to model how she would respond to the prompt. She pauses and looks at the ceiling, sighing and talking aloud to herself about the prompt. She tells students, "You don't have to write in sentences. You can write bullets, just ideas." She begins to do so on her laptop, casting a glance at the screen. "Here's what I'm thinking about." Maja shows students that her initial draft is more like speaking, recording on the page. She makes funny faces, looking into students' eyes rather than at the keyboard as she types in response to the prompt. Her goal is to write something hyperbolic and humorous to help relieve tension:

> *How embarrassing! James would rather die than be seen with his crazy white mom. So she's treating his life FOR-EVER riding that crazy old bike—rusty, rickety, whatever. And then she isn't looking at anyone and everybody's staring at her.*

Maja's goal is to make the writing process look like fun. More specifically, her goal is to relieve the intense pressure that she has noticed her Generation 1.5 students often feel about writing. She wants to model the process of informal writing and how to avoid getting stuck based on a desire to write in perfect, formal written English.

Eventually Maja shows how her writing could become a claim:

> *As a young boy, James is embarrassed by his mother's unusual behavior, but as a grown man, he appreciates her integrity, which shows his maturity and deepened understanding of his mom.*

This vignette reveals Maja's understanding that multilingual students often need clear modeling of how to engage in academic language tasks, like using writing to brainstorm ideas for later academic arguments. She shows her students how to write using multiple registers, or levels of formality, and how to engage authentically in writing that generates ideas.

Building on what we have already discussed about shaping a responsive environment, this vignette demonstrates how responsive teachers like Maja model and support ways to use language as a resource in academic and social contexts so that ELL students can engage in responsive literacy communities. Communities like these provide opportunities to apply language knowledge and get real-time feedback from others. A responsive community also allows for cross-cultural and interpersonal, authentic learning. What does it mean to support language as a resource in academic and social contexts? In particular, what language understandings might be useful for supporting ELL students?

***Key Understanding:* Academic language requires demands different from those of social language, yet the two intersect. Attention to language forms (oral, written, social, and academic) is necessary to support students in an authentic literacy community.**

This chapter focuses on how responsive teachers can better understand their students' various language abilities and support their ability to respond to a range of language demands—oral, written, social, and academic. As a key starting point, we need to be sure to assess the range of students' academic language proficiency in spoken and written language for the range of students (from multilingual to newcomers). This means explicitly teaching academic language and providing supports, like modeling, that help students engage in academic language use. To do so, I suggest ways to plan for these supports by understanding differences and connections between ELA content objectives and English language objectives. Later I discuss ways to provide students with authentic opportunities to use academic language, including strategies for helping students build academic oral language.

Authentic Modeling to Show How to Use Academic and Social Language as Resources

Starting with Authentic Literacy Tasks

Let's think back to the image of the new ELL student sitting in the corner of the mainstream ELA classroom. Let's consider myths about *when* and *how* ELL students should take on aspects of ELA learning. Consider the following myth:

Myth: ELL students should delay engagement with authentic literacy until they master conventions of spelling, vocabulary, and grammar.

Reality: This approach is problematic because we know that adolescents are often motivated socially. In fact, effective teachers of ELL students support authentic experiences using language from the start in supportive participatory literacy communities "organized around aspects of literacy such as spoken word poetry, open mic events, bookstore events, writers' collectives, and book clubs, and [they are] chosen spaces . . . organized outside of work and school settings or they are alternative and supplementary spaces for learning" (Fisher, 2005, p. 117). This kind of community is important because it provides real-world interactions and reasons for language use, which have been shown to have much stronger learning potential than decontextualized information about language.

Of course, creating an authentic literacy experience doesn't have to be outside the classroom; we want to support and attend to students' social and academic reasons for using language in order to promote learning within our classes.

Understanding Academic and Social Language Distinctions

As a starting place, let's get on the same page about a key definition: What is *academic language*? Typically, academic language refers to language used in schools, those words and terms that can be found on tests or in textbooks. Another way of defining academic language is as the language specific to a discipline. In English language arts, for example, academic language might be specific content, like the transition structures used to frame an argument. It can also mean the academic vocabulary and syntax used in particular genres, words such as *metaphor*, *simile*, and *synecdoche*.

Social language, by contrast, is the language students use with peers (sometimes referred to as BICS, or basic interpersonal communication skills), which ELL students often develop quickly when learning additional languages. "Academic language" (sometimes referred to as CALP, cognitive academic language proficiency) is usually more complex and decontextualized than social language. In academic language, for example, sentence structures are often much more complex, with embedded clauses and abstract references. Unlike social language, which learners are more likely to pick up on their own, academic language often takes explicit instruction to learn, so learning academic language takes much longer than acquiring social language. One reason why: academic texts often use many words with Greek and Latin roots, whereas everyday language uses mostly Anglo-Saxon words (Freeman & Freeman, 1998).

Further complicating this discussion is the difference between spoken and written language, whether social or academic. Spoken language is generally interactive, as it relies on specific context clues, gestures, and expressions to make meaning. Written language, on the other hand, is often less personal and more edited: it's usually more abstract, not situated, and it often is reported rather than immediate (i.e., less often in the present tense).

These distinctions matter as we work to support ELL students and start to notice the abilities and needs they bring to our classrooms; further, we must consider how we unpack our own tacit language use and expectations.

Assessing Academic Language Proficiency: Considering Different Language Uses

These understandings of social and academic language need to inform how we assess students' language proficiency. And we need to consider the range of students we encounter in our classrooms, as discussed in the last chapter. Are students multilingual? How long have they lived in the United States? What kinds of schooling have they experienced and in which languages or varieties of English?

For example, the level of formal schooling in languages before English may influence academic language use—and provide us with some indication of students' knowledge of academic language in their home language. DeCapua and Marshall (2010a) describe how students with limited or interrupted formal education (SLIFE), may have specific needs based on differences between US schools (which prioritize independent, abstract learning for the future) and schools in "high context" cultures (that may value pragmatic, collectivistic learning). Their model for the mutually adaptive learning paradigm (MALP) describes the need for effective teachers of SLIFE to unpack assumptions and make academic language more explicit for our students through the following methods:

- Providing "immediate relevance and a strong interpersonal relationship" (DeCapua & Marshall, 2010b, p. 167);
- Combining culturally familiar aspects with the new aspects of in-school learning and academic language tasks; and
- Using written as well as oral modes for learning, such as transcribing students' oral responses; having students write and speak in the same activity; or both saying and writing directions for students (DeCapua & Marshall, 2011).

Social interactions are key, then, as a means of promoting academic learning. Further, DeCapua and Marshall (2010a) note that we can link some students' past learning models with a US model by incorporating "both shared and individual responsibility routinely," bridging "oral and written modes consistently," and promoting academic tasks while using "familiar language and content" (p. 54). Part of doing this work of bridging past schooling and language use with current schooling and language use requires us to contemplate the language we expect and teach in ELA classrooms in the United States, particularly academic language.

Learning more about academic language can help us work better with all students, but especially with ELLs. Let's begin with these two ideas:

1. There are key differences between oral and written language use.
2. There are also key differences between "registers," i.e., levels of formality in different contexts.

In other words, the split between academic and social language is clean and distinct. Multiple registers of both oral and written language extend from social to academic, complicating any simple way of thinking about these terms.

In fact, understanding the range of ways we think about academic and social language can be useful for all students. Especially with new ways of communicating emerging in online spaces, understanding the ways language changes in different contexts is critical (and can sometimes be confusing for us as teachers!) For example,

Register: any specific rhetorical practice (sometimes referred to as "style") or variety of language that has specific linguistic features (lexical and grammatical) associated with it; it's often associated with the level of formality used in different situations or with different audiences, purposes, or settings (e.g., business-speak).Written and spoken registers can differ, as spoken formal English may have different forms from written formal English. By a young age, even monolingual language users learn to switch between multiple language varieties relevant in different contexts.

NOTE: Spoken and written registers have differences and take different levels of planning. Speakers can use intonation and gestures. Speaking usually happens face to face and relies more on the context. In general, written registers are more formal.

are blogs "academic" or "social"? Or are they a mix of the two? Further confusing our students, we may assign blogs, yet, in an attempt to have students write in more formal or academic language, apply an essay-style rubric that asks for a formal, or static, register that doesn't allow students to use more informal features such as first person pronouns or contractions.

Teaching academic language has been a vital part of what's considered best practice in working with ELLs. Sometimes this work suggests that we should offer ELL students more explicit instruction because they speak varieties of English that are different from the content area textbook. However, this way of thinking leads us to the following myth:

Myth: Some students "speak like the textbook" (coded to mean academic language) and others don't. Those who do are smarter and better able to succeed in the classroom.

Reality of Oral and Written Language Differences: We all speak somewhat differently than we write. Written work is often highly edited, and even in unedited writing the rules for written language have been more stable because formal schooling has privileged rule books and grammar guides (developed with the rise of the middle class in Great Britain in the eighteenth century). But the rules in these guides also change and can be contradictory, so much so that even our trusty "grammar checkers" offer conflicting and/or erroneous advice (Curzan, 2014). Unlike English spelling, which has fairly agreed-upon rules, "grammar" or "style" "errors" are much more fluid than these grammar guides suggest. Yet, at the secondary level, critical thinking about these language authorities is not often part of our curriculum.

Oral language is much more in flux. Even academic oral language can change quickly and can depend largely on the context. And in different parts of the country, different oral language constructions are considered "standard" by listeners. For example, "The car needs washed" will be understood as standard oral English for many white English speakers in central Pennsylvania and some midwestern regions, but certainly not in others.

There are other constructions considered standard in oral conversation by most listeners across regions. Consider how most of us use "each student should grab their book" in oral English, though many English teachers will still correct written versions to "Each student should grab his or her book" or "Students should grab their books." Yet we know that this form is functional in oral English, and there's a good reason that singular *they* ("gender-neutral singular pronoun for a known person, used as a non-binary identifier") was voted word of the year for 2015 by the American Dialect Society and is now accepted by the *Washington Post*'s style guide.

So what do we know so far? Academic language rarely comes naturally to anyone, even native speakers, and context can define what meets the academic language bill. Further complicating matters are the ways levels of formality, or registers, function within both academic and social uses of language. That's one reason we have to pay special attention to the ways "academic" language plays out differently in oral versus written contexts.

Noticing How Different Contexts Lead to Different Uses of Language

Noticing how students use language in different contexts can help us better understand the range of students' language use. At her private middle school, new teacher Meghan notices that some of her students, who are from Vietnam, "speak fine." She didn't realize they weren't native speakers until she saw how they used verbs in their writing. Immigrants from Vietnam may, for example, use tense and aspect differently, because verbs aren't conjugated in Vietnamese, and tense and aspect are often determined from context. In contrast, student teacher Lindsey found that a student with good writing skills struggled with oral language, a problem that become apparent during a formal speech. Lindsey also describes how grading papers led her to discover what she calls an "ESL student," a classification she didn't make until the tenth week of teaching that semester. And when she noticed issues in the writing, she grappled with how to classify this student:

> We do have an ELL student. Well, she's not even ELL. It's just English is her—it's just more ESL, I guess, or English is her second language. But she knows it very well. I guess maybe she is ELL, but she's really advanced. Sometimes funny things do happen in her papers that don't happen in other people's papers as far as grammar goes. They're not things that I automatically related to her language issues, but [her experienced cooperating teacher] definitely did. [The teacher] pretty much lets it go. She'll correct it. She'll write the corrections and things, but she won't mark the girl down for it as much as she might somebody else.

Lindsey's situation is familiar to me and may be familiar to you too. Early in my teaching career, I began to notice students' different language abilities in reading, writing, and speaking contexts, and I probably used deficit wording, much like Lindsey does here, and was confused about how to classify what I was seeing. As I began to learn more about the differences in language use, I did a better job of planning for ways to anticipate and assess these differences along the way. I also realized the importance of avoiding initial assumptions about who was a "native" speaker and who was multilingual—and that all students need help navigating between social and academic language expectations because they have to juggle such a wide variety of language demands. I also learned that some of my savviest, most advanced language users were often multilingual. That helped me avoid the

Case of "Generation 1.5": Understanding the Range of Language Use Experiences

We face complex challenges in our mainstream classrooms surrounding these issues, and nowhere is that more true than with Generation 1.5 students—an increasingly mainstream and overlooked type of ELL student. Generation 1.5 students are often defined as students who have immigrated later in life (but before teen years) and may use oral language similarly to native speakers (sometimes called "ear" learners) but whose writing may have nonnative characteristics since they have not studied English academic language in grade school. As they routinely blend in with peers, they may bristle when labeled as "language learners," hide their language use from others, criticize their own language abilities, and/or carry memories of feeling stigmatized by being pulled out of classes for "ESL" services. This quotation from a recent article captures this phenomenon: "Teachers would start telling me about this group of kids they didn't know what to do with, that weren't the immigrant kids, the newcomer kids. Many of the kids had been in the states their whole lives, but clearly they didn't have the language they really needed to participate meaningfully in school" (Olsen qtd. in Bear & McEvoy, 2015).

Generation 1.5 students exemplify the range of students we may encounter as teachers, underscoring the need for both oral and written language knowledge. This further highlights the importance of teacher-student relationships as well as peer-to-peer identities. As linguistically responsive teachers, we can use sociolinguistic understandings of language to guide instruction, noting both the demands of different forms as well as the social and academic language implications of any given classroom interaction.

For me and for focal teacher Maja, for instance, the term *"Generation 1.5"* helped us understand our students' strengths and identify areas for support and future learning. Maja learned about the term when attending a session at the 2004 TESOL (Teaching English to Speakers of Other Languages) conference, which she was drawn to because of the session description: "Do you have students who aren't really ESL bilingual? They're kind of Americans, but different?" She was intrigued by the different needs "of Generation 1.5" students compared to those of ESL students, whom she was originally trained to teach. Although Maja had noticed that many of her "ESL teaching strategies" were also relevant for Generation1.5 students, strategies do change depending on students' confidence in oral and written language, as well as their past schooling experiences. While some newcomer ELL students may prefer opportunities to write before speaking, Generation 1.5 students generally seek opportunities to use their strong oral social fluency before sitting down to write about complex ideas. These students may feel the need to fit into strict molds of "correct" academic English while they're writing, even though jumping immediately into academic English might stymie their thinking processes.

Unlike Maja, I had little training in "ESL" strategies or language teaching as an early English teacher. Like Lindsey, I struggled with surprises as I uncovered the complexities of my students' various language abilities. What may be hard to realize for some of us, according to Maja, is how many students in large metropolitan areas may not be "native" speakers: "Native speakers are probably not going to be your clients. Your clientele will be 1.5. They're your bread and butter. They're our American kids, not foreigners as some teachers might imagine." But before we can truly know where students may need additional scaffolding for their language learning, we must understand how students are using oral and written English—both social and academic.

need to use "ESL" or "ELL" as a label to indicate that someone was more or less advanced. Instead, I learned to research the language resources students have so that I can understand my students' multiple language understandings and needs.

Providing Supportive Instruction for Varied Language Demands

Unpacking ELA *Content* Objectives vs. English *Language* Objectives

The issue of Generation 1.5 students highlights the need to consider both our content and our language objectives in teaching the English language arts, because we use our understanding of the academic and social language demands in a given ELA task to shape our instruction.

This approach has primarily been described as the Sheltered Instruction Observation Protocol, or SIOP (Echevarría, Vogt, & Short, 2003), and promoted by WIDA, an organization promoting academic language in education (see https://www.wida.us). The SIOP model asks teachers to plan for both content and language objectives as they support English language learners in mainstream classrooms. Eliana, a district ELL coordinator, describes how she sees content area teachers benefiting when they use SIOP to shape their objectives in the classroom: "You invest in a way of instruction that actually benefits all students."

SIOP resources contain many detailed checklists for planning, which can be overwhelming to a teacher at first (see the annotated bibliography at the end of this book for some key resources). In my experience, it's worth learning about this system because the approach reminds us to provide context for language use through multimedia, images or visuals, realia (objects from everyday life), hands-on manipulatives, and demonstrations—all techniques that many ELA teachers already use.

For me and for others, one of the biggest takeaways from the SIOP model is that articulating *language objectives* when we teach helps make the academic language understandings, or language demands, explicit for all students. A language objective is a way to articulate the academic language goals for a lesson, or the academic language students will need in order to access the content and meet content standards (see Table 4.1 for an example).

Although these objectives may not seem that different from the goals that most ELA teachers set on a daily basis, separating out a language objective can help us better identify and support the specific language tasks in a type of ELA learning. For example, oral language often uses more casual transitions, such as *because* to signal relationships between claims, whereas more formal transitions are needed in academic writing, such as *moreover*, *for instance*, *therefore*, or *thus*. Making the language-specific aspects of our lesson explicit for ELLs is especially important so that they extend their understandings of how oral and written language use may be distinct in a variety of social and academic contexts. It also helps many teachers

Table 4.1. Standards in Relation to Content and Language Objectives

Content Standards from CCSS	Content Objective	Language Objective
CCSS.ELA-Literacy.W.9-10.1 Write arguments to support claims in an analysis of substantive topics or texts, using valid reasoning and relevant and sufficient evidence. CCSS.ELA-Literacy.W.9-10.1.c Use words, phrases, and clauses to link the major sections of the text, create cohesion, and clarify the relationships between claim(s) and reasons, between reasons and evidence, and between claim(s) and counterclaims.	Students will be able to draft body paragraphs for their argumentative essays.	Students will be able to **use transitional phrases** to link or clarify claims and evidence in their paragraphs (e.g., "as an example" or "after all").

note which kinds of language demands (i.e., specific aspects of reading, writing, listening, speaking) they may be using in a lesson (and perhaps not even be aware of), and how they are supporting those language demands within the lesson.

Steps for Developing a Language Objective

Ask yourself these questions:

1. What academic words, concept words, or key vocabulary will students need to use or understand? Are technical words or phrases needed? Will students encounter words that mean one thing in a social context and another in an academic context (e.g., *argument*)? Are there connections or differences in how the ELL students' other languages may use academic vocabulary to signal similar concepts?
2. What language skills are required—oral, written, listening, and/or reading? Sometimes language functions, such as *to describe*, *to analyze*, or *to explain*, can provide clues to the language structures ELL students need to master.
3. What specific grammar or language structures, such as syntax, are specific to the genres or pieces that students will encounter (e.g., compound sentence structures; passive/active voice; transitional phrases)? What is the "voice" of the writing and how do these structures contribute to it? Are these structures similar or dissimilar to structures ELL students know from other languages or from social uses of English?

Supporting Authentic Opportunities to Use Academic Language

Let's consider how experienced teachers support academic language learning in the classroom to promote authentic opportunities for using language. Here are some tips:

1. *Avoid decontextualized language study.*

Often when we first hear about "academic language" or "language study," we imagine students need more grammar exercises, daily oral language (DOL) opportunities, or vocabulary study. But research tells us to avoid generic, unresponsive activities like DOL with both ELLs and other students (Jimenez et al., 2011). Even though ELL students may need daily practice with oral English, avoid DOL-type activities that focus merely on proofreading, error hunting, or other activities unrelated to actual language use in context. These kinds of disconnected language study activities usually don't provide rigorous learning opportunities. Instead, grade-level-appropriate activities need to include authentic ways for students to use oral and written language with their peers and other audiences. Consider ways to provide immediate relevance (as noted by DeCapua & Marshall, 2010b) and build on the familiar as you introduce academic language content through real-life connections, demonstrations, and visuals.

In Practice: Example of Authentic Oral Language Practice in Maja's Class

Key Practices in This Vignette

- Modeling and practicing syntax for specific language demands
- Linking oral and written language use
- Providing contextualized language engagement
- Engaging students with authentic learning tasks
- Applying learning over time

As she introduces ways to develop arguments, Maja has her students practice oral language structure for argumentation using contextualized language study. She tasks them with persuading their parents to buy them new shoes and has them try out conjunctive resources (such as the subordinating conjunctions *although*, *because*, and *since*) that account for the rhetorical situation and audience.

Maja begins by modeling how to use conjunctions and then has students practice in pairs: "Although I still wear these shoes you purchased in April, I want another pair of shoes that provide better support for my feet." She explains that the students' goal is to get what they want by acknowledging both their audience's needs (in the initial dependent clause that uses a subordinating conjunction like *although*) as well as their own desire for and rationale justifying new shoes. By having students first practice the oral rhetorical effect of the conjunctive phrase initiating the request rather than simply saying, "I want new shoes," students can see how the syntax of argumentation often uses structures that acknowledge multiple perspectives in order to provide support for the argument.

Similarly, later in the semester Maja will have students practice and reflect on the professional language used in job interviews versus informal discussion with colleagues. Together the class decides that instead of using "big words," they need to use appropriate academic, professional, and/or technical words. Throughout the year, they continue to apply understandings of how audience and context intersect with levels of formality in both lexical (word choices) and syntactical (structural) decisions in English language use.

2. *Plan for activities that promote higher-order thinking skills related to content and language objectives, not just drills in academic vocabulary.*

Literal questions about vocabulary or content are easier for us as teachers to generate without preplanning than questions about more in-depth, higher-order skills. That means we have to help students engage with academic language beyond simply learning academic vocabulary. For example, they may need to understand the structures used in higher-level questions or to understand key ways in which discourse in ELA is structured, such as ways to incorporate evidence or clearly construct an analysis.

To support these higher-level skills, Vogt, Echevarría, and Short (2010) also suggest preplanning for both content and language objectives. For experienced teachers of ELLs, these objectives are often internalized and tacit; however, for most new teachers of ELLs, it can help to explicitly identify the objectives to make sure they are providing language supports. In the In Practice example that follows, new teacher Cole does just that. He first preassesses the academic language students already know related to the terms *analyze* and *theme*, since his content objectives are related to a language objective that focuses on the language function of analyzing in speaking. In his preassessment survey before the unit, some questions focused on content, such as how students feel about the role of English in relation to notions of success, a key theme of the unit, and he asked students, "How do you feel about English? How important is it to your life?" He also asked, "When you are told to analyze literature, that means to . . ."; "When you are asked what the word *theme* means, you say . . ." He found that students struggled to describe what *analyze* means, because they referred to it as "scan[ning] over the reading," so he set objectives to help them understand the concept of analysis through examples and modeling what analysis looks like, including the types of higher-order thinking students need to do in order to analyze, and the language they need in order to express those analyses effectively.

In Practice: Example of Planning Content and Language Objectives Based on Academic Language Understandings

Key Practices in This Vignette

- Providing authentic context for language use
- Promoting meaningful engagement
- Supporting written and oral language demands

New teacher Cole designed a unit for a sixth-grade language arts class that includes students' discussion of texts in response to a central theme: "What is success?" The unit ends with a Socratic seminar to provide an authentic context for students to have an engaging, academic conversation about the readings.

One content objective is for students to be able to discuss the texts orally in a Socratic seminar using citations from the literature to support their points. Based on this objective, Cole identifies the word *cite* as relevant academic vocabulary for the unit since students need to understand what *to cite* means in both their written work as well as in oral academic discussion.

Because he knows that academic language includes addressing syntax related to the academic language demands, Cole plans objectives based on what he expects to hear in the Socratic discussion when students cite from the texts. In his written and oral models prepping students for the discussion, Cole develops students' understanding of a language objective: *Students will be able to engage in academic conversations about texts and use syntax (prepositional and adverbial phrases) that connects their ideas to a source.*

Cole realizes that at this stage, students don't necessarily have to know the underlying grammar terms, but they would benefit from some sentence starters and examples to help them practice that kind of phrasing. To meet this language objective, he models to help students practice the skill of citing using specific syntax. For example:

- *<u>In the</u> Diana Nyad TED talk, Diana's age of sixty years was an obstacle for her, but that didn't stop her.*
    - OR: "In [source], [description of information that provides evidence], [my reflection/interpretation].
- *<u>After</u> reading the two stories of Brian and the three doctors, and reading the success articles, <u>I see</u> . . .*
    - OR "After reading [source], I see [my takeaway based on this reading that supports my answer].

3. *Consider all types of language use in objectives, including written and oral academic language.*

For example, students can share content and language objectives orally with a partner. This social opportunity provides a time to use academic language in an oral context, and can give you time to assess how well students comprehend those objectives. Using academic language orally builds a sense of accomplishment for ELLs, who may then feel more confident that they understand and can use more complex language. You can further support this kind of understanding by providing visual representations of the academic language and/or objectives being used (either on the handouts, on the projector, or on the wall).

In Practice: Using Oral Academic Language and Making Connections to Everyday Language

Key Practices in This Vignette

- Using verbal and nonverbal cues
- Connecting academic and everyday language use
- Using ongoing, embedded language study with real-life examples
- Distinguishing between oral and written language use

Maja talks a lot about formal academic language and informal language, and she often models both orally before asking students to incorporate academic language into their writing. She gives students a list of "dead words," such as *a lot, nice*, and other vague words.

She has students analyze language that they care about by reviewing the school's cell phone policy, looking at how the Latinate words function by providing very specific information. She notes how the Anglo-Saxon words (*put, make, take*) are more ambiguous. Maja also talks about the history of the English language: "Did you know that 75 percent of English words are from the Battle of Hastings (like *children* or *fish*) and that some of our "fancy" words come from Romance languages?" She asks students to compare "the fire was extinguished" (fancy vocabulary) to "the fire was put out" (everyday vocabulary).

As the class looks again at the cell phone policy, which states that personal phones being used will "be confiscated," Maja's students say, "Oh! If you just said 'my phone was taken,' the verb *taken* isn't clear." They now understand that the informality of oral speech, combined with a lack of interpersonal context, might make "my phone was taken" too ambiguous, whereas the policy's use of a Latinate word, *confiscated*, clarifies the meaning, because *taken* can mean both "confiscated" and "stolen."

This type of discussion paves the way for discussing academic words in literary contexts. Maja builds off of students' past discussions about language use in a poem, such as comparing *second to last* to *penultimate*, to describe the latter as a very "tight" academic word. Knowing another language, she says, especially a Romance language, can help with understanding and using an academic vocabulary.

Other teachers use visuals, such as annotating with color or imagery, to help students unpack the academic language that helps us understand how writers make meaning in a text. For one chapter in *Miracle Boys*, Ann introduces the concept of symbolism by posting images around the room that represent key symbols students will encounter in that chapter. She asks students to stare at the images—a dog, a jogger, a stork, a newspaper—then arrange the images in their own sequence, and finally share with peers to summarize what they understand. Each small group presents its logic and understanding of the use of symbolism in that chapter to the rest of the class.

4. *Review and assess how students did and/or didn't meet the content and language objectives.*

It's also important to review how we are building on and emphasizing purposeful language objectives that are going to be vital to ELA learning in our classes over time. One of the primary benefits of having clear language and content language objectives is that we can better assess how ELL students are engaging with the varied language demands in our ELA classes. Given the range of language demands and the different levels of proficiency ELL students bring to the classroom, we need to consider how students are using language across multiple contexts. How flexible is their language knowledge? One way to support students is by assessing levels of understanding and how these understandings should inform our teaching. Recursive opportunities for language use can help deepen and solidify student learning.

For example, in the earlier vignette about Cole's class, his attention to language objectives helped him focus on citing in an oral academic discussion. When he assesses student participation during the Socratic seminar, this objective will help him know whether he needs to reteach and/or expand that language skill in future activities and units. In the next unit, for instance, he might build on this objective by determining whether students can use these structures in more informal small-group discussion when prompted to cite evidence. In other words, he can see if students are now able to access those structures more tacitly, without the written preparation they performed in the prior unit.

Noticing how our language objectives were or weren't met (as well as when content objectives weren't met and what language demands may have gotten in the way of success) can help us plan the skills we need to model more explicitly for students and how much ongoing practice students will need.

In Practice: Recursive Modeling Based on Students' Language Needs

Key Practices in This Vignette

- Modeling appreciation of language
- Providing ongoing practice and connections
- Using students' prior knowledge

Maja identifies some academic words that are critical to her classes, such as *juxtaposition* and *irony*. She teaches academic vocabulary like *juxtaposition* because it helps students understand a key concept that is necessary and useful in the kinds of analytical writing they are routinely asked to do in the curriculum. She uses it recursively in students' reading and writing activities, and she checks to see if students can use it in their writing and discussions effectively. She provides examples from professional writing in different genres. For example, she shares professional reviews of Twilight and Harry Potter films that use the word. She talks about different situations in which a word like *juxtaposition* is used, asking students to notice and consider, "How would you use it in different situations?" She asks students to consider related words they would use in different contexts, like breaking up with a boyfriend or girlfriend. She models how to savor a word, using the metaphor of chewing on words like food, to feel the word, let it marinate, and savor its unique flavor. Throughout the year, Maja initiates conversations using academic language learned earlier in the semester to extend experience in areas where she thinks students need review and more practice with application.

5. *Support written academic language by building on students' language backgrounds.*

Over time and based on research (see Ortmeier-Hooper, 2013a; 2017), I've learned to challenge my assumptions about what students know about our ELA content area structures, particularly those related to academic writing and the writing process. For example, one area of academic language that native speakers may understand from early school days is the structure surrounding writing workshop and peer review, an understanding that may not be as clear for ELLs. Fu (2007) notes specifically that to even the playing field for ELL students, we need to teach some specifics surrounding writing processes and writers' workshop. Enright (2013) describes supports ELL students may need in writing processes, including modeling of language use and an articulation of the purposes behind graphic organizers (p. 40).

Part of apprenticing ELL students into the writing community, however, requires you to build on what you know about their language backgrounds as you show them how academic writers use resources and manage the writing process. Sharing models along the way—both oral and written—can help ELL students engage in the process. Using students' knowledge and writing samples as models of specific writing discourses (e.g., the discourse of analysis discussed in the In Practice section on pp. 86–87) can also help them understand how academic writers collaborate, use resources, talk through ideas, and revise language use based on specific audiences.

Building on ELL students' own writing in many forms has incredible potential to support academic language understandings. One way to do this is to consider how first language writing can promote ELL student learning. Encourage students to write in their first language because such writing supports thinking and expression. It's important to note that all academic language development needs frequent writing time—both formal and informal writing in different formats—and ELL students writing in their home languages can help achieve that purpose. For example, keeping a reading response journal rather than answering worksheet questions supports ELL students, according to Fu (2007), because it gives them more freedom to respond and asks for more comprehensive responses.

But what if you can't read the first language writing of your students? You have a few options. You can use length to make some judgments, which encourages students to write more than a few lines. Also, Fu (2007) describes how sometimes another student can summarize for you the main ideas in a peer's writing, or how the writer can include images linked to the writing. She further encourages us to be aware and supportive of nonlinear writing development, since students may be able to employ a biliterate voice, one in which they use both languages to help them make sense of the content (see Alvarez, 2017).

To support ongoing development of academic language, build on what students know in their first languages and explicitly teach academic language structures in English. As we can see in Maja's example in the vignette starting on page 86, students may (or may not) have access to academic language in their first language, so we need to assess their levels of understanding and support them as they add new academic language into their repertoires.

In Practice: Building on Students' Language Backgrounds to Support Academic Language Objectives

Key Practices in This Vignette

- Varying instruction based on specific, contextual language learning needs
- Recognizing language learning opportunities for all students
- Noticing patterns in specific groups of students
- Using students' learning as a resource
- Using an understanding of register to inform teaching
- Providing models for specific language demands (e.g., analytical verbs for syntax)

Maja shares her approach:

> If most of my students are Gen[eration] 1.5, I will pay special attention to the use of conjunctions and sentence structure although, I must admit, every student, regardless of their linguistic background, needs this kind of support. For example, many Gen 1.5 students have trouble with the use of subordinate conjunctions such as *whereas* and *although* and conjunctive adverbs such as *nonetheless, accordingly, thus,* etc., because they don't hear them used often, they haven't been asked to pay attention to how they are used in a text, or they are unclear about their meaning.
>
> Another linguistic feature of Gen 1.5 students is the use of verbs in that they tend to use vague verbs such as *get, put, and take* in academic writing. For this purpose, I provide all of my students with a list of analytical verbs compiled by a former student of mine who was a Gen 1.5 student. Thus, students gain access to and learn how to discuss a novel by stating, "*Things Fall Apart* examines the relationship between . . ." as opposed to "*Things Fall Apart* talks about . . ." At the same time, I feel that Gen 1.5 students merely magnify the general needs that all students have, so although 1.5s may need a little more support, by examining sentence structures and analytical verbs, every student benefits, thus no student feels singled out. [See the List of Analytical Verbs on p. 87.]
>
> For my students who speak in the African American vernacular, many of whom may not be African American but who identify with this vernacular, we discuss code-switching. I don't use this term, but instead focus on formal vs. informal registers, such as "How do you greet people at a party of teenagers?" vs. "How do you greet people at your grandma's birthday party?" My students understand that we vary the way we speak depending on our audience, which is a perfect segue into the Rhetorical Triangle, so that students are able to discuss how the purpose and the presence of a variety of audiences steers and shapes our discourse. Again, while my students who mostly speak in this vernacular may highlight the need for the discussion of registers, every student regardless of her background needs awareness regarding the use of registers.

As Maja notes, this need to understand registers includes speakers of stigmatized varieties of English, monolingual speakers learning the discipline of ELA, and ELL students.

Below is a list of analytical verbs that one of her former Generation 1.5 students generated while in Maja's class. This student looked up synonyms for analytical verbs and grouped words with related yet varied meanings in order to expand her analytical writing repertoire. Since then, Maja has shared this list—often on request—with other students. They find that it helps them take on the discourse of academic analysis, because understanding analytical verbs supports the reading of analytical prompts and critical pieces, as well as edit their own analytical writing.

List of Analytical Verbs

Conveys
Cements
Chronicles
Explores
Evokes
Invokes
Indicates
Addresses
Implies
Employs
Incorporates
Juxtaposes
Marks
Signifies
Reveals
Exposes
Encapsulates
Captivates
Develops

Expresses
Creates
Demonstrates
Illustrates
Portrays
Depicts
Reflects
Displays
Mimics
Delineates (outlines)
Targets
Softens
Harnesses (controls)
Inserts (e.g., a profusion of alliteration)
Secures
Envelops
Engulfs
Spins (a web)

Highlights
Stresses
Accents (accentuates)
Heightens
Echoes
Resonates
Emphasizes
Intensifies
Strengthens
Affirms
Reinforces
Solidifies
Enhances
Underlines
Amplifies
Expands
Magnifies
Concentrates
Dwells

Lingers
Ponders
Confesses

Negative Words:

Weakens
Diminishes
Disassociates
Minimizes
Lessens
Disconnects
Detaches
Belittles
Curtails
Depreciates
De-emphasizes
Softens
Contradicts = Belies
Admonishes

Supporting Intersections between Types of Language Uses

Making In-/Out-of-School Connections

Recognizing the distinctions between oral and written language and between academic and social language demands doesn't mean we shouldn't also make connections between language use types and contexts. Over time, I've learned to ask myself more explicitly about students' oral language use—both academic and social, e.g., what areas of the ELA classroom align with students' use of oral language both inside and outside of class? For example, we are all familiar with the ways some authors use vernacular and dialogue in their writing, but even academic writing can involve concepts of "voice." In some ways, this can be problematic given the distinctions between oral and written language use. However, the concept of voice in academic writing can be helpful as we encourage our students to move beyond robotic, overly structured ways of using language.

As a case in point, Maja helps her students embed oral language into their academic writing. Although she doesn't teach dialogue (because her classes don't focus on creative writing), she helps students see how oral language is sometimes useful "embedded in snippets or something and that helps them develop their own voice—their writing voice—so why not?"

Sometimes this understanding about oral–written connections can help ELL students build confidence in switching between language types. Maja describes how she supports these connections with some ELL students in her class who are reluctant to write:

> [Some of my multilingual students have told me that they have] trouble expressing themselves in writing . . . and don't like writing that much. It doesn't get them as far as their speaking does and so I think that there seems to be such an enormous gap—and I emphasize the word *seems*—between how they speak and how they imagine academic language to be. They just feel it's unbridgeable, but I don't think it is. I think a good teacher should encourage their students to . . . write the way they speak maybe at first, and then through the drafting process kind of slowly, help them . . . flesh out their thoughts and translate them into academic English. . . . Because they are such great oral communicators that you need to exploit that. They need to exploit that and try to crystallize and develop their thoughts as much as possible in speaking and [in an] elaborate drafting process, and kind of help them translate that onto the page. But I think that their confidence just declines when they write and so teachers really, I think, need to help them gain as much confidence as possible and make writing as unrepulsive as possible by constantly asking them to write.

Another way we can help make these connections is through the participatory literacy communities discussed at the beginning of the chapter, such as literary magazines, newspapers, and other extracurricular literacy activities. The next In Practice case, focusing on a literary magazine, reminds me why I embraced advising the school newspaper. My multilingual student writers enjoyed exploring ways to use and understand flexibility in language as it shifts with audience and purpose. Having a specific genre and style guide, like the Associated Press (AP), enabled us to talk about how language shifts in different contexts and audiences—for instance, why AP style doesn't use the Oxford comma when one's English teacher might require it.

In Practice: A Literary Journal Provides Authentic Language Engagement

Key Practices in This Vignette

- Engaging students with real-world language use and community connections
- Writing for authentic genres and audiences
- Positioning students as experts in a participatory literacy community (PLC)
- Valuing multilingual language use

As editors and writers for the *Ricochet Review: Annual Poetry Journal*, students pair up with experienced poets in a mentorship exchange. Student poets are positioned as "apprentice poets" who work with "master poets" and editors from another literary magazine. As faculty advisor, Maja helps students collaborate with published adult poets, produce the magazine, and observe the ways other literary magazines interact with the public.

This literary magazine doesn't follow the typical high school model that accepts and publishes most writing. Instead, the journal provides

> opportunity for high school poets to hone their craft through a guided, workshop-style collaboration between experienced, published, and talented master poets, who understand the art of poetry and how to convey it. Side by side, apprentice and master, Padawan and Jedi, pupil and teacher will learn from each other and create brilliant written tapestries published in each issue.

As students take on the role of magazine editors, they edit poetry with attention to how detail can transform meaning. What makes this use of language so authentic is that students aren't just writing for class. "These are now published poets," notes their principal, who supported the project after the students' faculty advisor took him to a reading for another school's literary magazine. "They're not just taking classes. They've learned how to express themselves, they're building this community, this fellowship. It's no longer an experiment, it's a reality."

The students are a mix of language learners at various stages, many of whom are multilingual. Their in-depth understandings of language are often acknowledged in the themes for the magazine. For instance, the third issue focused on poetry in translation, as Maja explains, "not only from other languages but other forms of art. The languages featured are Bosnian, French, Hebrew, Khmer, Mandarin, Romanian, Serbian, Spanish, Swedish Tagalog, and Urdu." So far all issues have acknowledged the ways in which poetry enacts complex ways of using language and making meaning. Maja describes how the second issue was inspired by Oulipo, "the French literary movement applying scientific principles to the craft of poetry, and the first issue focused on the art of the monostich."

Each issue celebrates with a launch party publicized on social media. This evening event brings together past and present contributors, editors, authors, and teachers. Students perform the poems for the public audience, and their work surprises and amazes their parents and families. Having poetry lauded in a public venue enables students to share their writing expertise and capitalizes on their understandings of language—both oral and written. Students also take an active role in raising money on sites such as GoFundMe and DonorsChoose to keep expanding and supporting their endeavors.

Their work develops through the process of collaborating with poets and one another. Sharing with the community (both in written and performance formats) also lets them communicate in a new way with their families, community members, peers, and other writers.

The connection to the discussion of academic language is that student poets apprentice in the creation of specific poetic forms, learning techniques for sharing those forms in a written format and in the performance venue. They also work alongside others who can speak to the processes, such as the drafting, revision, and editing, that are entailed with producing poetic language. In addition, they learn about genres for writing to raise funds, communicating about an event to the press, and publishing their website.

Validating Student Language: Recognizing What ELL Students Add to the Conversation

The examples of ELL students excelling outside of school based on language use should serve as a reminder that we need to advocate for students who may not recognize their own strengths or abilities. As we consider ways to plan more explicitly for developing students' academic language and related language objectives in our classrooms as a means to support all of our students, it's important to note that ELL students add much value to our classrooms. Eliana, district ELL coordinator, comments on what I have also noticed: "Students with varied language backgrounds can make structural comparisons based on their language knowledge."

In particular, Eliana describes what ELL students often bring to our mainstream classes:

- Greater potential for understanding linguistic structure (metalinguistic awareness)
- Accelerated literacy development specifically in students learning to read in two languages that share a writing system (e.g., English and Spanish)
- Significant advantage compared to monolingual students in the development of general executive processes and cognitive problem-solving skills, including conceptual categorization and selectivity and identification of similarities and differences (including verbal and nonverbal domains)

Validating these understandings that our ELL students bring to the classroom can further help them share their assets in the classroom community and beyond.

Recognizing Value in Language Variation: Why and How to Address It

As teachers, we know the importance of incorporating academic language into the curriculum. Another area to be sure we consider is the way we treat what we see as nonacademic language or other English language variations.

Experienced teachers and research tell us that criticizing students' varieties of English is counterproductive, as with the teacher who says, "That's not English. You won't speak that in this classroom." As described earlier, experienced teacher Ruth instead sees students' language as "real and rich language with complex and documented grammar." Maja too understands the value of "code-switching" in English:

> Students need to be able to code-switch and they should know standard American English because when you go from the Midwest to New Orleans or Boston, that's something to fall back on. We need it. We need it, but we need both the varieties and standard American English. It definitely should be cherished.

Like these teachers, I've learned that English language variation in our classrooms is another opportunity. My studies have shown the ways specific language concepts such as style-shifting and code-switching can enable teachers to adjust their consideration of what is "appropriate" in order to avoid deficit perspectives of students and students' language use (McBee Orzulak, 2013, 2015). To keep from responding in an alarmed way when students don't produce what we perceive to be academic language, we need to remind ourselves how we shift in formality in our own writing. This can help us frame the academic language to use in peer responses as we model what counts as "good" language by unpacking myths about "good" language and helping students command the language relevant to a particular register.

You may have heard several terms used to talk about language variation: for example, *code-meshing*, *style-shifting*, *code-switching*. As we think about academic language objectives, code-meshing is a useful concept. Young, Barrett, Young-Rivera, and Lovejoy (2014) use the term *code-meshing* to refer to "using two languages in the same context, such as alternating between languages in a single conversation or using more than one language in a single piece of writing" (p. 31).

This language use could include meshing at two levels: intrasentential (alternating within a single sentence or utterance) or intersentential (alternating between two sentences). Young et al. advocate for using the term *code-meshing* rather than *code-switching* (at least as defined by most educators) because code-meshing is a better description of the blurry line between informal and formal language use in media communication as well as in academic and political discourse (2014, p. 78).

So what does it mean to address code-meshing in your classroom? Many students will understand this concept when you compare it to the differences in their writing when they participate in online spaces. Because students (including ELLs) have internalized some norms for interacting online (e.g., using a term like *G2G* ["got to go" or "good to go"]), we can use this as a basis for discussions about when and how to use different language constructions. Doing so can help students both better navigate these spaces and connect this understanding to code-meshing their multiple languages.

Code-meshing is what we hear Maja doing when she merges informal and formal oral registers to model academic language for her students in the vignette that opens this chapter. Here's a different type of situation in Maja's classroom where she chooses to draw on students' informal oral language while reading *Hamlet*:

> Hamlet says to Ophelia, "Oh, I never loved you, blah, blah," and my students said, "Wow! Treated! She's treated. He totally treated her life." So kind of inserting those, maybe, slang words that speak to them [e.g., "treated" as *insulted*], and that's how they know *Hamlet* is not about some old play. It's about life.
>
> I think that in terms of the language I use, it's like a combination of academic and informal. I feel that if you just speak academically, you just really turn them off, and so you do need to speak their language as you . . . delicately insert academic lingo.

In this example, Maja models her own code-meshing to help students engage with the themes of literature. They can also use this concept to help them see the different structures for English in different registers.

Next Steps: Understanding Language as a Resource for Academic and Social Contexts

Overall, this chapter discusses the need to consider a wide range of language demands in our teaching, specifically how to support academic language learning. This includes ways to move beyond thinking solely about vocabulary in relation to academic language and focusing instead on other areas such as syntax, discourse, and audience awareness. Developing language objectives for our teaching can help us better plan for instruction in academic language and the complexities of language use in its written, oral, social, and academic forms. An academic language focus benefits all students in the classroom, and we gain much from the added value of ELL students' abilities to incorporate knowledge from other languages and registers into the class. Perhaps even more important, discussing the ways language use is often linked to power and access—since definitions of "appropriate" language can be bound by social mores, assumptions about race and culture, and stereotypes—can open up critical conversations in our classrooms.

Getting Started: Questions to Ask Yourself

Considering Language Demands and Resources

1. How do you use formal and informal language strategically for specific contexts and audiences?
2. What language objectives would support key content learning in your class (this week, in this unit, across the year)?
3. What strengths do students bring with their understandings of various language demands?
    a. Academic? Formal?
        - Written
        - Oral
    b. Social? Informal?
        - Written
        - Oral
4. What are the language demands that you see students struggling with?
    a. Academic? Formal?
        - Written
        - Oral
    b. Social? Informal?
        - Written
        - Oral
5. What authentic literacy opportunities do you provide for your multilingual students? What authentic literacy opportunities could you advocate for?

Chapter Five

Supporting Respectful and Rigorous Reading Opportunities

"Can anyone help me out here?" Ann asks.

During a unit focused on reading YA novel Crossing the Wire *by Will Hobbs as a whole-class anchor text, many Spanish-speaking middle school students raise their hands when their teacher asks for help with an unfamiliar term in Spanish. Students, some of whom have been traditionally quieter in the class, pipe up with a response. Throughout the unit, many of these students become the experts in the room, translating and explaining Spanish terms used and cultural experiences described in the text in relation to the plot of the novel. Their understandings enable their peers without this knowledge to better comprehend the text.*

Later, when students have opportunities to work in stations to produce projects based on multiple options, several ELL students decide to work together to create a Spanish–English dictionary of phrases from the book, which they share with their classmates.

In this moment, the sixth graders in Ann's ELA class tap into opportunities to engage in the respectful, rigorous reading community she has worked to develop for the range of students. This is just one example of how her text selections shape this community and also influence students' writing. Underlying this selection, as well as others throughout the year, is Ann's determination to create a "culture of reading" with her students, inviting multilingual students' expertise and considering her text selections carefully based on what is available in her district.

This chapter builds on what we know so far about developing responsive classroom communities by applying understandings from previous chapters to meet three common curricular challenges that intersect with reading. These curricular challenges relate to creating respect and rigor in our classrooms and acknowledging that we may face these challenges in new ways with our ELL student readers.

- First, we may face the challenge of ensuring that *what* we teach—texts—and *how* we teach open up opportunities to engage in a culture of reading. And how do we accomplish this for a range of multilingual students without isolating students due to reading level or experience?
- Second, we face the challenge of letting go of teacher-centered instruction, even as we offer appropriate rigor. Given the range of multilingual students in our ELA classrooms, how do we avoid overly simplistic instruction that segregates or bores some students or, on the other end of the spectrum, overly sophisticated instruction that overwhelms others?
- Last, we face the challenge of helping students negotiate among the multiple language demands of diverse reading, writing, and speaking.

In the face of these challenges, the overarching question is this: how might we create rigorous reading opportunities for our ELL students while at the same time continuing to challenge *all* the students in our classrooms? Specifically, what language understandings should shape the kind of curricular planning we need to do in order to answer that question?

Key Understanding: **To meet the challenge of creating respectful, rigorous reading communities in ELA classrooms, responsive ELA teachers consider their specific multilingual students as they (1) purposefully select and frame texts to shape the community; (2) scaffold reading through front-loading and multiple active engagement strategies; and (3) support reading with purposefully paired writing tasks.**

As described in earlier chapters, fostering communities of practice (Faltis & Wolfe, 1999) by creating responsive spaces means helping students become part of the academic community and making sure they are active, valued participants. Creating a strong classroom community through meaningful interactions between students and content, as in Ann's classroom, helps students engage with academic learning. This is especially critical for ELLs because a strong classroom community fosters desire—and the expectation—to participate and to learn from others. In these responsive classrooms, ELL students know that their knowledge will be built on in classroom activities. They also know there will be different ways to communicate that knowledge in class through varied writing, listening, speaking, and performative activities. Further, responsive teachers acknowledge their desire to learn more from students and therefore identify and plan for the academic and social language demands of the reading in the curriculum.

To meet the curricular challenges we face in trying to plan these types of communities, this chapter takes us into classrooms where ELA teachers maintain a rigorous curriculum but at the same time provide a welcoming environment for ELL students. Specifically, you'll see how responsive teachers consider and integrate the following aspects of their curriculum in order to create stronger reading communities:

1. Framing and selecting texts to meet the challenge of creating responsive reading communities in heterogeneous classes
2. Planning varied, student-centered, active learning interactions to meet the challenge of supporting ELL students through authentic, scaffolded literacy learning
3. Making connections between reading and writing tasks to meet the challenge of helping students engage with multiple language demands

As you review the sidebar related to principles taken from the *NCTE Position Paper*, you'll notice that ways of selecting and framing texts are not necessarily new for our best practices in the English language arts. But having ELL students in our classes can help us affirm and advocate for these effective practices in new ways.

Reviewing Reading Principles from the *NCTE Position Paper*

Reading

- "Introducing classroom reading materials that are culturally relevant" using themes and texts of varying levels of difficulty to support students
- "Connecting the readings with the students' background knowledge and experiences"
- "Encouraging students to discuss the readings, including the cultural dimensions of the text"
- "Teaching language features, such as text structure, vocabulary, and text- and sentence-level grammar to facilitate comprehension of the text"
- "'Front loading'" comprehension via a walk through the text or a preview of the main ideas, and other strategies that prepare students for the topic of the text" (e.g., provide opportunities to read a more accessible text first) (p. xiv)

Thematic Framing and Selecting Texts to Support ELLs

In Maja's class, her ninth graders are exploring the theme of identity throughout the year. Through this lens, they investigate internal vs. external conflict; peer pressure; and the impact of culture, such as family, religion, history, and language, on identity formation. In quarter 1, their anchor text is Marjane Satrapi's *Persepolis*, a graphic novel/memoir about an Iranian girl growing up in Iran during the 1979 Revolution. She is conflicted about being loyal to her secular family or to an increasingly religious Iranian society—eventually becoming a rebel who immigrates to Austria.

This graphic novel introduces the theme of identity through both words and drawings, thus helping students understand that text can involve both. Above all, the novel offers compelling story lines about coming of age and the fall from innocence to experience, as well as rich and engaging illustrations. To support this anchor text, Maja has students engage in document-based questioning (DBQ), which focuses first on a collection of nonfiction texts, authentic pictures, and maps of Iran. One of the articles, for example, examines the popularity of plastic surgery in Iran as a result of women having to cover their bodies but being allowed to show their faces, a concept that fascinates students.

For quarter 4, students read *Othello*, on the heels of Chinua Achebe's *Things Fall Apart* in quarter 3. Students notice that both protagonists, Othello and Okonkwo, have names beginning with *O*, are of African descent, and are tragic heroes. Once students learn that a Shakespeare tragedy usually ends with the death of the protagonist—as well as of all the other main players, and often in a bloodbath—they are hooked. Love, hate, murder, race, evil are a recipe for an engaging read, especially through the theme of identity: Is Iago Satan? Why is Othello so naïve? What makes Desdemona so gullible? Maja parallels the reading of the text with watching a Globe Theatre stage production of *Othello* and the movie *Othello* with Laurence Fishburne. *Othello* is the highlight of and a perfect culmination to the school year, and a day doesn't go by without the students asking, "Are we reading *Othello* today?"

What Is DBQ?

Document-based questioning (or data-based questions) is referred to as DBQ and has been promoted by the College Board and www.dbqproject.com as a way to develop inquiry-based units so that students' argument writing is coherent and evidence based. For example, students use writing to help themselves figure out what they think as they explore texts with open-ended questions such as "Is Mayella powerful?" as they investigate race, class, and gender in *To Kill a Mockingbird*, or "What is the biggest obstacle to reaching the American Dream?" in *The House on Mango Street*. The underlying purpose of DBQ is to have students rely less on pure recall of information and instead learn the analytical skills of exploring big ideas and questions in relation to analysis of new (often multiple) documents, or sources.

Framing Texts Thematically to Support ELLs

Let's start with how Maja selects and frames texts based on thematic planning, a fundamental way to support ELL students. First, Maja begins with the graphic novel because this kind of text enables the class to practice key analysis strategies while also learning to make meaning from both the written and the visual texts. Maja focuses, for example, on images and realia like the novel's cover, and she models how to make connections based on cross-cultural understandings. Then she uses students' understandings to make connections across classic literature, young adult literature, and other texts. The texts she's chosen all deal with issues of culture as well as identity, which encourages students to explore concepts recursively.

Thematic planning can provide useful connections between students' experiences, texts, images, and other content instruction. Big ideas like the one Maja has chosen offer a conceptual framework that allows for individual choice but also leads to student engagement and the need to investigate in multiple modes. These thematic connections between different modes (i.e., text and visuals) are useful, especially with ELLs, because visuals add to the meaning-making potential of a text and help students to unpack key concepts through both written and visual cues. Connecting with other content areas also helps students recognize a cross-curricular context, which helps to solidify (and delineate) critical academic concepts and language.

Similarly, Ann's sixth-grade class, described at the beginning of the chapter, includes themes that will engage that age group, particularly those that include a focus on community and relationships between people. Many of the texts have specific themes that appeal to middle school students: being misunderstood, having a cause, or considering whether something is right or wrong.

How might you do the same in your own classroom to help all students, but especially ELLs? You can begin by asking questions like these:

- What are the big questions at play that could link to other texts and experiences? (e.g., What does it mean to do the right thing? What is freedom?)
- What visuals or realia can you use to help teach your content?
- How can you collaborate with teachers in other disciplines or content areas?

While a thematic approach has proven to be successful with most ELLs, it's important to note that some students, depending on their schooling background, might consider student-centered, constructivist approaches as "not teaching." It helps to clarify with your students your objectives for using a student-centered approach. For instance, you might need to explain to them the ways thematic instruction helps students make connections across disciplines, texts, languages, cultures, and experiences. Research into second language acquisition helps us see why this is so important. When acquiring new language skills, we must make comparisons and connections to our current understandings. For example, a cross-curricular approach can help students understand concepts in more depth; it also provides more opportunities for cross-cultural sharing, which increases student motivation and engagement. Thematic units can also create opportunities for a range of readings and activities at different reading levels. Kucer, Silva, and Delgado-Larocco (1995) describe how themes in multilingual classrooms improve the overall curricular conversation. Integrating understandings is especially important for language learners, which is why thematic topics are important; themes can help students make generalizations and build on concepts across and within the curriculum.

Selecting Materials to Build Responsive Reading Communities for ELLs

Part of developing solid thematic instruction includes attention to the types of texts we select to engage with the theme. A theme like Maja's focus on identity connects to students' experiences and allows teachers to select from a broad range of available texts. Brown (2007) reminds us that language and culture are vitally interlinked, and this notion becomes even more vital when we teach diverse concepts and texts to ELLs. As we make curricular choices, it's important to consider their cultural implications. These questions, as adapted from Brown (2007, p. 213), are a good place to start:

- Does the text or lesson avoid negative stereotypes of the students' cultures or any other cultures?
- What cultural values (customs, belief systems) are presumed by the activity or text?
- If the text or activity pushes students out of their cultural comfort zones, is it doing so empathetically and respectfully?
- Are specific language features connected to "cultural ways of thinking, feeling, and acting"?
- How does the text or activity include students' experiences with other cultures and/or capitalize on students' strengths in terms of background experiences?
- Are there myths about language and/or culture that may need to be addressed to prepare for the text or activity?

These questions will also help you focus on appropriate text selection. For example, you want to select texts that will lead students to share literature and personal stories. Even when we don't have complete freedom to select our texts, we can pair short and long readings strategically. Plus, there may be additional opportunities to provide options if the school structure allows for students' silent choice reading or literature circles and small groups.

Part of how we build on students' strengths in the classroom is by connecting our materials to their experiences and using materials to connect students to one another. Maja describes the ways her material selection affects her teaching in a multilingual classroom:

> Another avenue into a unifying conversation is the books/novels we teach; they span many cultures—languages, religions, and other backgrounds. The curriculum must acknowledge and reflect the diversity of the students we teach. For most students, teaching a memoir or a novel that reflects their cultural backgrounds is like '"coming home,"' which is a great opportunity for bonding with students.

Both texts and our approaches to texts allow us to position ELL students as contributors. Ann, for instance, selects books from those available in her district to provide multiple points of connection for her middle school students. She bases these choices on what she learns about students' reading histories. From her beginning-of-the-year survey, which asks, "What was the last book you read?," she's discovered that her students often name children's titles, or explain that they don't like to read. She knows that her course often introduces students to their first young adult novel.

So Ann picks books to start the semester that have appealed to her students in the past. Her goal is to create a culture of reading, and she tries to select books that students relate to. She wants them to be excited about books and see connections to their own experiences, though she also finds that her own excitement about a book strengthens her students' interest in it. One year she started with Jacqueline Woodson's *Miracle's Boys* for the class to read together as an anchor text. Many students could relate to having lost a parent and other issues related to families and living in an urban setting. Another example of a whole-class anchor text that has engaged students is the one mentioned in the opening vignette, *Crossing the Wire* by Will Hobbs, which includes descriptions of the main character's life in Mexico, death of a father, and a journey to the north, and some students are able to share their own stories that connect to the text. The novel contains potentially political issues, as well as concepts Ann's students can relate to. As Ann chooses these books, she continues to grapple with questions about whether texts include potential stereotypes.

Ann also considers the format and topic of a book when deciding whether it should be read as an anchor text by the whole class or as a choice book read in small groups. For instance, as ELL students read Paul Fleischman's *Seedfolks* as a whole class, they often find the thirteen chapters written from thirteen points of view to be a manageable format. Students get to read about different cultural perspectives in shorter chunks and study how chapters use point of view to develop characters across the book as a whole. This format enables the class to chart out characters from the different chapters. The class reads one chapter aloud, then students read one on their own, and then they read in small groups, applying reading strategies together and on their own.

Similarly, *Wild Girl* by Patricia Reilly Giff has been popular as a small-group choice book. Ann has found that students can relate to a Brazilian girl who faces moving and living with grandparents. The main character is unsure on the first day of class in the United States and feels frustrated when placed in a lower-level math group—when she had been a star math student in Brazil—and then faces the embarrassment of wetting herself because she struggles to communicate that she needs to go to the restroom.

"Okay, but what about me?" you may be thinking. Because every classroom includes its own unique range of ELL and other students, how should you make your text selections? In *Book Bridges for ESL Students*, Suzanne Reid (2002) describes the ways teachers should provide opportunities for student choice, seek to avoid stereotyping, and remain aware that student preferences may be based on personality as well as cultural differences.

According to Reid (2002), language learning opportunities from a book—whether read independently or as a whole class—should include opportunities to

- Read it
- Write about it
- Discuss it
- Compare it

How might this look using a whole-class text for cultural and language learning opportunities? To build understanding and maturity about cross-cultural issues, some teachers use Linda Crew's *Children of the River* as a whole-class read. The book describes the tensions of the protagonist as she tries to fit in with American culture and her struggle to hold on to traditional values from her Cambodian background. It also describes the perspective of her football player friend, who is drawn to her and brings his own assumptions about life and culture to their friendship. Writing about, discussing, and comparing the characters' perspectives provides students with touchstones and extensions for their own cultural identifications and assumptions. For instance, native-born American students who are not multilingual learners may see themselves in both comparison and contrast to different characters. They may begin to identify assumptions they have made about gender, culture, schooling experience, and/or national identity.

Selecting the right book for a whole-class read (and the right books for small-group/choice reading), though, is complicated, especially in terms of how the text might position students in relation to other students. This can complicate book selection and also lead us to think about ways to frame and use a given book. For example, for a German American student reading about the Holocaust, you might want to address stereotypes by discussing how people have multiple identities and can choose to respond differently to national or historical trends, just as some Germans chose to be bystanders and others to be rescuers within Nazi Germany (e.g., curricula developed by Facing History and Ourselves offers frameworks for analyzing visual images and stereotyping as well as identity charts to help students consider their multiple identities in relation to others).

Expanding the Book List: Providing Multiple Entry Points Related to Language, Culture, and Interests

Expanding our schools' book lists is especially vital for ELL students because we may find that the titles reflect a narrow range of reading levels and perspectives, which can lead to lack of student engagement or accessibility and limited possibilities for rich thematic unit development. For many teachers, this means expanding our own reading repertoires in order to discover high-quality books that will not only engage ELL students but also fit into the themes of our curricula. Luckily, there are many resources that can help us in that discovery.

1. The links provided by the "Motivating ELL Student Readers" section of the website www.colorincolorado.org/article/motivating-ell-student-readers provide principles and ideas for selecting texts that will motivate your students.

2. Book awards:
   The Pura Belpré Award is presented annually "to a Latino/Latina writer and illustrator whose work best portrays, affirms, and celebrates the Latino cultural experience in an outstanding work of literature for children and youth." See www.ala.org/alsc/awardsgrants/bookmedia/belpremedal. Or check out www.ala.org/yalsa/booklistsawards/booklistsbook for a complete searchable list of national awards in the Teen Book Finder database from the Young Adult Library Services Association.

3. Websites with ideas and booklists for diverse reading include:
   a. www.entubiblioteca.org (en tu biblioteca)
   b. http://weneeddiversebooks.org (We Need Diverse Books)
   c. www.everythingesl.net (everythingESL)

4. *Text Messages:* A podcast describing young adult literature:
   ReadWriteThink.org and NCTE sponsored Jennifer Buehler's podcast, *Text Messages: Recommendations for Adolescent Readers.* This resource provides podcasts with descriptions of young adult literature as well as lists of the books described in the podcasts. Specific podcasts relevant to expanding literature related to culture include:

   - Latinx examples: www.readwritethink.org/parent-afterschool-resources/podcast-episodes/latino-literature-teens-30972.html

   - International selections may also be relevant to your classroom, such as www.readwritethink.org/parent-afterschool-resources/podcast-episodes/international-books-teens-31028.html

Planning Varied, Student-Centered, Active Literacy Interactions

In addition to considering which texts we use and how we can frame them, supporting ELLs means engaging students in classroom interactions as a way to foster communities of practice in responsive reading communities. This means finding ways to empower ELL students as readers in the community.

Part of creating these active, rigorous communities means letting go of teacher-centered instruction, which too often doesn't account for ELLs, and instead planning for strategic classroom interactions that include ELLs. Research shows us that in secondary classrooms content instruction is often driven by teacher-talk, which is especially problematic for ELL students because mainstream teachers often don't modify how they deliver content orally with consideration for ELL students' needs (see Brooks, 2015). Furthermore, ELL students who might be verbally engaged in ESL classes are instead often placed in mainstream classes that don't tailor oral opportunities to their needs—for example, teachers may not model what a response would sound like. Students also can be frustrated when they don't understand what's going on, for example, when a teacher uses puns or parentheticals (Harklau, 1999, p. 45). Activities that just ask students to jot down knowledge for checked homework can be problematic too, as ELL students may be able to find the answers but not really understand what those answers mean.

For ELLs, engagement through a literacy community that encourages active participation is crucial; otherwise, true language acquisition opportunities are being lost. This active participation requires key front-loading, modeling, and scaffolding of student responsibility. What does it mean to create this kind of community? You might start by thinking about these questions regarding how you structure your classroom:

Are the activities I include interactive and rigorous?

- Do students have opportunities to contribute, opportunities for choice (in inquiry topics, reading, and writing), and opportunities to have voice and responsibility?
- Are students engaged in activities integrated socially among different ability levels and backgrounds (both linguistic and cultural)?
- Are students' experiences reflected and included in the curriculum?

Are the texts I include encouraging an active, responsive community?

- What types of texts are available in my classroom and school or community libraries? Are there multicultural books? Is a range of cultures, languages, classes, genders, and authors represented?

- What can I add to make the books at my school more representative of the ELL students in my context?
- Which books am I familiar with and can recommend to students? Where are the gaps in my reading?
- How am I leveraging students' heritage languages to enable access to community and academic content?

Note that the last four questions also link to issues of text selection. Why are the questions in this section about active engagement? One reason that text selection and framing of those texts was a starting point for this chapter is that these choices can make a difference in how students participate in cooperative or active learning.

What gets in the way of letting go of a teacher-centered approach, especially in mainstream classes with ELLs? Teachers can worry that a more democratic classroom will lead to chaos or disorder, or that students won't be supported when they are struggling with reading. However, this is not the case for responsive teachers who plan carefully. We know that responsive ELA teachers often structure meaningful literacy learning through various groupings such as literature circles and workshops with mixed groups of students, and through providing (and sometimes letting go of) specific scaffolds to support ELL students, as well as all students in ELA classrooms.

Front-Loading Instruction: A Key Scaffold to Developing an Active Reading Community

Just as thematic planning promotes student learning through big ideas and essential questions, responsive teachers plan to front-load different reading and writing activities based on an understanding of students' reading, writing, listening, and/or speaking abilities in English. Techniques for front-loading, according to the *NCTE Position Paper*, include "comprehension via a walk through the text or a preview of the main ideas, and other strategies that prepare students for the topic of the text" (p. xiv) (e.g., provide opportunities to read a more accessible text first). This emphasis on front-loading reminds us that moving toward active learning does not mean dropping students directly into reading activities without clear scaffolding and modeling. In fact, "enticing activities," or ways of luring students to engage with an overall theme or content, can pique students' interest and pave the way for understanding; for example, teachers can begin by "presenting the main point of a text in clear, simple, understandable language" (Ariza, 2010, p. 65). Remember Maja's first day activity of having students engage on a personal level with provocative quotations from the range of quotations pulled from texts they would read throughout the year? This activity initiated students into being part of Maja's active community of readers, foreshadowing how her ELA class engages them in making personal connections to texts, connecting themes across the year, seeing relevance in literature, using evidence to share ideas, and engaging in cooperative learning to make meaning as a class.

You can also front-load by providing activities that set students up for successful reading of a text. The following vignette shows how Maja front-loads—by planning a range of activities, from modeling to whole-class discussion to small groups, that engage students as readers before they even start reading the text itself.

In Practice: Maja Front-Loads a Novel

Key Practices in This Vignette

- Front-loading using visual learning and realia
- Connecting to past and future learning, including language use experiences
- Activating social connections
- Engaging students with choice and questions
- Connecting to other disciplines and understandings (cultural or social capital)

When Maja teaches *Things Fall Apart*, her students do the following to set the stage for reading the longer text.

STEP 1: Examine and analyze the layout of the novel by looking at the book's cover and format. According to Maja, "This is a great tool for making predictions and inferencing, and it follows Bloom's Taxonomy in three moves":

1. First, students notice layout features without the obligation to make inferences. For example, they observe that the front cover features a mask or a head, which is upside down. They usually have a rich discussion about whether it's a head or a mask.
2. Then they make connections between the book's format and its title, such as wondering what falls apart during the story. They also examine the cover colors and study the information on the back cover: the author blurb and the summary.
3. Maja then has the class open the book to the epigraph:

Turning and turning in the widening gyre
The falcon cannot hear the falconer;
Things fall apart, the centre cannot hold;
Mere anarchy is loosed upon the world.
—W. B. Yeats, "The Second Coming"

Here, students notice that the title of the book is included in the epigraph and share their schema about what "The Second Coming" might refer to. Then they notice that the subject of the poem is in the second line, so the first line acts as a preamble—a phrase that Maja and her students call a "condiment," whereas subject-verb pairs are "lean meat." They look up the word *falcon* on Dictionary.com and discuss the difference between falcons and eagles or another bird and draw inferences from the information that the falcon is a predator, which leads them back to the title again. Students have another discussion about the word *anarchy,* and Maja helps them make connections with other words such as *arch* and *hierarchy* and the prefix *an-*, as in *anaerobic* or *atypical.* They also discuss how the verb *loose* is used.

STEP 2: Ask anthropological questions. Maja provides students with a set of standard anthropological questions that one of her colleagues found in an anthropology textbook. The class discusses the word *anthropology* to understand the purpose of anthropological questions about culture such as, "What is considered fair and unfair? What do people talk most about? Who runs things in the home and in the community?" These questions and others help students examine a variety of cultural aspects, such as burial practices, what is considered funny, wooing practices, and wedding ceremonies. In pairs, students choose the one question that serves as the lens through which they and their partner will read and annotate the novel together. They also write critical reading journals (analytical writing) and make oral presentations based on this question. In this way, each pair of students becomes an expert on a particular cultural aspect of the novel. Students enjoy this activity because they are able to make connections with their social studies class, an example of a cross-curricular activity.

STEP 3: Make connections to nonfiction and other disciplines. If there is time, students choose an excerpt from their world studies text that pertains to colonialism or any other aspect of the novel.

In the vignette, we see how Maja uses front-loading to develop students' cultural and social capital. This setup allows students to build on understandings from their own cultural experiences, as well as on their interests as adolescents in relationships. Students smile and laugh as they consider wooing practices, and ask each other and later the text, "What is wooing?" and "What does it mean to seduce?" Students are able to choose their own questions to explore the text, which draws on their curiosity. When they begin to make connections to their own answers on the initial anticipation guide and in the initial course discussion on traditional West African cultural perspectives in *Things Fall Apart*, they exclaim, "Whoa!" as they make new connections. They encounter new ways of reading text as they explore for meaning and along areas that interest them, rather than focusing solely on what the teacher wants them to notice.

Maja's goal is to build a strong active academic community, which she sees as important for multilingual learners in particular. Their engaged interest in a subject can help them persist when they encounter challenging language or texts.

Planning Ways to Scaffold Reading Instruction and Encourage Student Engagement

Because our ELL students will come into our classes with different reading abilities and different reading challenges, we need to be particularly thoughtful about our choices for designing reading interactions. How should in-class reading be structured so that it's most helpful for these students? A recent study focused on long-term English learners reminds us that variation in how we approach reading is particularly important for ELLs. If, for example, we use only one main strategy for reading in the classroom, such as reading aloud to students or round-robin reading, strategies that are common in ELL-populated classrooms, students won't necessarily learn what to do if they are reading alone and independently (Brooks, 2015).

Think-Aloud Modeling: Teacher Scaffolding and Gradual Release

As we provide scaffolds for reading, one approach that has been shown to help students is a think-aloud modeling of reading (e.g., Wilhelm, 2012). Simply put, a think-aloud is when you, as teacher, read a section out loud and talk through your own processes in approaching a text. This approach can promote a culture of reading by demonstrating to students what other readers may do while reading a text, thus encouraging students to try new approaches themselves. You can model reading for students and then have them work in smaller groups or independently to apply the strategies. The goal for many whole-class think-alouds is to help students move toward independent practice.

Using think-alouds doesn't mean you can't also use some well-structured whole-class reading with grade-level texts to provide access for ELL students (Vogt et al., 2010). The key is to make sure your structure also provides practice opportunities rather than relying solely on teacher-driven language use (e.g., the teacher's oral reading).

Here's a tip: Select excerpts for an occasional, purposeful out-loud reading, or consider how you are providing a gradual, strategic release of responsibility as you teach students how to use specific strategies. Mix the teacher-led or whole-class reading with other kinds of reading. While your inclination might be to read everything aloud to help ELLs, that's a sure way to frustrate your higher-level readers and keeps readers who may be struggling from practicing with grade-level texts.

A Range of Approaches to Reading: Creating an Active Reading Community

A range of approaches can be used to help structure class engagement with reading and responding to texts. Consider implementing both teacher-led and student-led strategies because using an assortment of approaches is most helpful in working with ELLs.

1. Teacher-Led: How can teacher-led reading provide scaffolds for student reading?
    - *Purposeful Teacher-Led Read-Aloud:* Planning read-alouds for specific parts of a text allows you to model effective intonation, helping to capture nuance within the text. This can be critical for ELLs, especially when you're modeling how key concepts are revealed through a genre's style and rhythm, or even modeling how to grapple with new vocabulary within the text.
    - *Teacher-Led Reading with Planned Student Participation.* Here are options for teacher-led in-class reading that can be used for strategic purposes. When you plan for student participation, ELLs are more likely to understand the purpose of specific activities.
        - Page and Paragraph (see Vogt et al., 2010, p. 26 for details). This approach involves a strategic teacher-led whole-class reading that allows ELLs to see how you make meaning and want students to make meaning of a particular text. Basically, you start the interaction by reading a short passage aloud. Then, while the rest of the class is reading silently, you can work with a small group, alternating between their silent reading of a couple of sentences and your reading aloud.
        - Chime-in or Give-and-Take. In these approaches, students have a structure for participating in the reading at different points, usually after they have had a chance to read the text at least once. With Give-and-Take reading, you model dramatic pauses and inflection with punctuation and might call for choral reading or louder or softer reading at critical points (see McBee Orzulak, 2006). Students have to "jump into" the reading, usually at a pause from a period or comma, which can be intimidating for some ELLs but exciting for those who enjoy oral language. However, you can emphasize that students have a choice in how they participate by offering alternatives to oral reading, such as writing down key phrases for later reflective writing. You can also

emphasize how to pause dramatically to let new voices participate. As an alternative, Chime-in requires you to tap the desk of a student who then joins in orally as you read aloud along with that student. You can preplan a place for Chime-in with particular students to gauge their ability and comfort level with reading along with you.

    - Choral Reading. Reading together as a class can be a powerful experience. For ELLs, choral reading is an opportunity to have a voice as part of the group without pressure to sound "perfect." Group reading can include small groups that read a certain part of the text aloud to the class.

2. Student-Led: What are some options for student-led reading?
    - *Rehearsed Oral in Large Group.* The rehearsed component can help ELLs prepare for oral reading ahead of time, even for just a few minutes, to relieve on-the-spot pressure to produce oral language. Often teachers ask for volunteers, who then practice before the whole-group reading as the rest of the students work on a prereading task. As one example, you might remember that Maja's student-led discussions include a component of rehearsed oral reading as the facilitators select, practice, and present an excerpt to share during their discussion.
    - *Small Groups.* Working with one to three other students can provide a sense of safety and reduce the focus on performance (Vogt et al., 2010, pp. 26–28).
        - Page, Paragraph, Pass. This structure allows students in small groups to decide how much they want to read (e.g., a page, a paragraph, or nothing).
        - Equal Portions. Students read the same amount of text in small groups.
        - Small-Group Turns or Triads. Small groups control how they split up the reading. Reader, writer, and/or speaker roles can be assigned and rotated.
        - Partner Choral or Shared Reading. Pairing students to read orally together can help build their fluency and cooperative skills. Vogt et al. (2010) suggest making the underlying purposes clear to students and pairing mid-range readers with either lower-range readers or higher-range readers, because pairing the lowest and highest readers can lead to frustration. Creating "shoulder reading" ensures that the noise level doesn't

get too loud. Positioned shoulder to shoulder, students sit in chairs pointing in opposite directions so that they can turn their heads sideways to be face to face and have a conversation. Students then take turns reading, annotating, and/or discussing the text.

Pairing Tip: I used to list my students' names from highest to lowest reading level and then split the list in half and pair the student from the top of the first half of the list with the student at the top of the second half. With ELL student pairing, I also found it important to consider interpersonal relationships in addition to reading levels: what are the language use, gender, personality, and cultural dynamics in the classroom? These considerations sometimes led me to alter the pairings.

3. Individual Reading: What are options for individual assisted reading?
   - *Audio or Electronic Materials.* We need lots of approaches to best serve the needs of ELLs, and that can include use of audio materials (though be sure to note whether ELL students know how to use the technology and whether they will have access to the technology at home). E-readers enable students to look up and listen to words. Sometimes electronic resources can help students use multiple languages to understand texts.
   - *Post-its or Other Note Structures.* Students can use sticky notes to write down questions and unknown words. They can share these and write down additional notes in small groups or pairs and then share them with the whole class so that you can clarify key concepts and vocabulary.

You can also invite students to learn independently at different paces, as many of us know from reading and writing workshop structures. One way of offering ELLs multiple means of participation is through "curricular invitations" (Van Sluys, 2005), or a formal, thematic curricular structure that provides educational choices rather than scripted methods that require all students to follow the same path.

An example of a curricular invitation is a prompt for students to explore "Stories of Family(ies)" (Van Sluys, 2005, p. 65). Students begin by considering their own stories and then move on to teacher-provided resources related to family stories, such as picture books, chapter books, poetry, and video, to consider multiple stories and definitions of families. In their inquiry, students consider "What do I notice? What stories are told? Whose stories are missing?" along with other questions to help them further explore what the stories mean to them and others. Teachers should select resources that include various genres, a range of authors, and considerations of diversity—both linguistic and cultural. Students then have opportunities to share their responses with one another and the whole class.

Built on the understanding that learning is social, such curricular invitations enable students to take ownership of their learning while still participating in a scaffolded structure. In particular, Van Sluys describes how these invitations support critical practices, which can be applied to other types of literacy activities that ask students to

- Consider multiple viewpoints
- Disrupt the commonplace
- Focus on the sociopolitical
- Take action (2005, pp. 21–23)

Why is this kind of independent invitation important for ELLs? The underlying language understandings are that (1) offering choice can support motivation for learning; (2) providing links between language and culture can enable engaged learning; and (3) drawing on students' cultural and linguistic capital can encourage critical learning for the whole range of students in the class because they are able to learn from one another.

So, let's recap. Why does implementing a range of curricular interactions with texts help ELLs as readers more than relying solely on a round-robin style or teacher oral reading? Research shows that students don't necessarily pay attention during read-alouds, because they are often worried about how and when they will contribute. Many students will try to avoid this kind of reading, and ELLs do need practice with grade-level texts, not just opportunities to listen to their teachers reading. Planning for a strategic range of interactions with text can help you support students as they engage in rigorous yet supported reading tasks.

Planning Purposeful Cooperative Learning in Heterogeneous Classes

We need to find ways to make reading accessible as well as create reading communities through cooperative, active learning. As noted earlier, cooperative learning can help students improve their oral language development as they respond to texts (Soltero, 2011). Some traditional teachers, however, may balk when they see ELLs trying to work cooperatively when sharing hasn't been sanctioned by the class structure. It's important to note that cooperative learning, like mimicking, may actually be a culturally based learning style, not what some teachers might see as purposeful cheating. Therefore, more traditional teachers need to learn to pair ELL students with buddies and/or incorporate much more purposeful cooperative learning into their curricula.

Even if you, like many ELA teachers, are already a fan of cooperative learning, you can expand it to be responsive to ELL students by building on any cultural expectation for cooperation and perhaps even assigning a specific peer tutor or buddy to an ELL who might need one in order to fully participate in your class activities. Consider ways to encourage (and structure) collaborative talk versus instructional conversations. Some possibilities include planning for a range of combinations such as (1) numbering to structure which students talk together (Numbered Heads Together); (2) splitting up the text so that each student has a part to share or summarize; students with the same part first collaborate and then move into groups with all the parts to share the key takeaways from their section (Jigsaw); and (3) having students work independently to generate responses, then share with a pair, and then report as a pair to the whole group (Think-Pair-Share).

One cooperative learning structure ELA teachers use to help students engage actively with reading is literature circles, which can be designed with or without specific roles for each student. Literature circles allow students to share their literary responses and draw on their funds of knowledge in response to literature, especially multicultural literature, with personal stories (Roser, Martínez, & Wood, 2011). When literature circles include roles (such as Discussion Director, Vocabulary Enricher, or Artful Illustrator, as in Daniels [1994]), all students but especially ELLs benefit because the range of roles allows them to choose a role with fewer English language demands and build on other skills—such as visual abilities through interpretation of literature as an Illustrator—in an authentic language use context. The small groups also provide a safer space for using language. To prepare students for this kind of approach, you may need to model the roles required with a short reading and example of how each role might respond. Literature circles can also provide an opportunity for a class to explore a range of multicultural literature, which can in turn build on students' cultural understandings, similar to the way Maja's course of study provides students with access to discussions from multiple cultural perspectives.

Whatever your approach, it's vital to anticipate what might work in your specific context, with your specific students, and at a particular time of the year. In Ann's district, for example, the curricular structure for each unit has the whole class read an anchor novel, followed by each student picking a "choice" book to read in small groups. However, Ann has found that it often works better for her sixth graders to move into choice groups in the second semester, after the culture of reading has developed in the first semester through readings of several whole-class anchor texts. Anchor texts allow students to engage with a variety of whole-group, small-group, and independent activities. This paves the way for the second semester, when students work in choice-book literature groups of five to six students, in which each has a specific job or focus. Ann notes that, especially in a class with ELL students, assigning the right roles to students is important. Pairing can help some ELL students feel freer, but that depends on the student; some personalities are simply given to being off task. Ann helps students pick the roles in which they will find success.

Pairing Reading and Writing Tasks to Support ELL Students

Given the multiple language demands students will face, we need to acknowledge to ourselves *and* with our students that there may be differences between what they are reading and what they are being asked to write. Supporting them means understanding (and purposefully pairing) reading and writing tasks.

As discussed in other chapters, starting with what students are able to accomplish with language is crucial. This is where understanding what is meant by "academic language" can be helpful. As a reminder, academic language refers to grammatical structures that are specific to particular language demands—structures that might have a different function in another language context. For instance, understanding analytical structures and language, like transitional phrases that clarify claims, can be helpful for students like Maja's who are trying to write claims and counterclaims. Yet, students also need to learn that in literature, transitional phrases may be used to indicate narrative sequence as well.

Therefore, an important way to meet our curricular challenges is to notice what language structures are being used in the texts students are reading and in the texts students are being asked to write. Where are they connected? Where are the differences? How can you help students understand these similarities and differences?

Scholars who apply functional approaches to grammar have noted ways to help students develop grammar that works for the context in which they are writing, which includes analyzing that genre to see what counts as effective grammatical structure (Gebhard, Harman, & Seger, 2007; Schleppegrell & Go, 2007). In other words, we can help our students read like writers, by identifying the kinds of constructions writers use. For example, David West Brown in *In Other Words* (2009) explains how to unpack student writing to identify the underlying discourse patterns in certain types of academic writing, such as analyzing different types of sentence starters (e.g., his book describes lessons for "topic/comment" analysis that offer clear, in-depth examples of this type of linguistically based text analysis). You can do the same to help students see the similarities and differences between what they are reading in class and what you are asking them to write.

Here's one example drawn from Maja's class, where students are reading an excerpt from James McBride's memoir, *The Color of Water*, and focusing on individual sentences. In Table 5.1, the beginning of each clause or sentence appears in

Table 5.1. Charting the Patterns in the Students' Reading: *The Color of Water* Excerpt

First Part of the Sentence/Clause (Topic)	Second Part of the Sentence/Clause (Comment)
The question of race	was like the power of the moon in my house.
It's	what made the river flow, the ocean swell and the tide rise, but it was a silent power, intractable, indomitable, indisputable, and thus completely ignorable.
Mommy	kept us at a frantic living pace that left no time for the problem.
We	thrived on thought, books, music, and art, which she fed to us instead of food.
At every opportunity, she	loaded five or six of us onto the subway, paying one fare and pushing the rest of us through the turnstiles while the token-booth clerks frowned and subway riders stared, parading us to every free event New York City offered: festivals, zoos, parades, block parties, libraries, concerts. (McBride, 1996, p. 94)

the first column. Note how the words and phrases in this beginning position are important, both grammatically and thematically. That's why linguists sometimes refer to the beginning of a sentence as the "topic" or "theme," or what is being discussed in the sentence—e.g., the focus.

In the second column, you can see the rest of the sentence or clause. Usually this second part is where the writer develops the sentence's or clause's overall message, commenting in some way on the parts in the first column. In McBride's memoir example, you can see how the first parts of the sentence connect to the second part of the previous sentence.

Compare the chart of the written memoir excerpt (what students were reading) to Table 5.2, which shows Maja's oral think-aloud example from Chapter 4 in which she talked through her analysis of the text, and to Table 5.3, which shows Maja's more developed written argument claim when she modeled how she moved from the oral think-aloud into more formal analytical writing. In all three tables, the first parts (or topics) focus on people, but in slightly different ways. The written text has more formal transitions common in analytical writing, for instance, while the oral think-aloud relies more on shared context with the listeners.

The charting in these three tables shows different frequency and types of connection between sentences in the memoir text, the oral think-aloud, and the written analytical text. Often when we note that a paper needs work on "flow," it may have to do with how a student has structured the beginning of sentences—the topics, or ways of describing what is being talked about as the focus of the sentence or clause. Sometimes ELL students have internalized structures from writing in languages other than English that represent topics differently (e.g., not in the first position as in English, or referenced differently through allusions or pronoun differences). Or their writing may reflect a narrative structure or more oral format, as in Maja's think-aloud.

Table 5.2. Charting Patterns in Speech: Maja's Oral Think-Aloud

First Part of the Sentence/Clause (Topic)	Second Part of the Sentence/Clause (Comment)
How embarrassing!	
James	would rather die than be seen with his crazy white mom.
So she's	treating his life FOR EVER riding that crazy old bike—rusty, rickety, whatever.
And then she	isn't looking at anyone and everybody's staring at her.

In English we typically introduce new information in the second section of our sentences (or "comment" part) and draw on information that has already been introduced in the first part (or "topic" part). For example, in Table 5.3, we see how Maja's academic writing refers to "this deeper maturity" to start the second sentence that draws from the introduction of this idea in the second part of her first sentence. David West Brown (2009) describes how to teach students different patterns for creating cohesion through attention to the organization within their sentence structures by analyzing and paying attention to syntactical structures for "topic/comment."

To summarize, we need to analyze the structures important to the different kinds of writing we ask students to do compared to the structures of the texts we ask students to read, to make sure that students have models of the kinds of syntax we expect to see in their essay responses to literature, for example. Additionally, we need to model how to move from successful oral discussion to successful written structures. This is important because different types of writing have different language demands, as we acknowledge when we help students analyze mentor texts or examples in a genre. Scholars have noted the specific linguistic differences between different texts, even between different types of essays. Schleppegrell (2004), for instance, describes distinctions between factual, personal, and analytical texts. Academic writing often requires complex syntax to express complex ideas. Generally, research shows that second language writers' sentences are shorter, have "fewer but longer clauses, more coordination, less subordination, less noun modification, and less passivation" than those of non-ESL writers (pp. 80–91). They often have fewer lexical ties, such

Table 5.3. Charting Patterns in Writing: Maja's Reframing of Oral Language into Written Claim

First Part of the Sentence/Clause (Topic)	Second Part of the Sentence/Clause (Comment)
As a young boy, James	is embarrassed by his mother's unusual behavior, but as a grown man, he appreciates her integrity, which shows his maturity and deepened understanding of his mom.
This deeper maturity	allows James to reframe how he perceives his mother's sometimes embarrassing behavior.
However, he	grapples with how he wants to manifest his own integrity as a black man in US.

as variation of words to link sentences, use of pronouns to signal earlier nouns, and use of synonyms for verbs.

Many ELLs struggle to make the move from the syntax of their interpersonal communications to the syntax required for the school genres of analytical and expository essays. Analytical and personal genres can be quite different in terms of language demands:

> 1. Analytical genres (e.g., account, explanation, exposition) often use nominal expressions to name arguments, and require subordination and condensation. For example, when Maja teaches students about subordinating clauses (e.g., "Although James's *mother* appears unhinged, *her* behavior reflects the inner strength needed to break down cultural expectations"), students can better connect their ideas using complex syntax.
>
> 2. Personal genres (e.g., recount, narrative) often include additive and temporal conjunctions, specific participants, and past tense verbs (Schleppegrell, 2004, p. 85). These genres are used frequently in everyday life to communicate information or job/school performance, but these structures are also more likely present in our literary texts. In Table 5.1, for example, we can see how the memoir uses "at every opportunity" as a conjunction to show time and frequency. ELL students need to develop the ability to reflect on experiences, such as describing their work over the semester in a Self-Reflection, with these types of temporal and additive conjunctions: "During first quarter, I learned that . . . ; I also learned . . ."

Helping students read and understand the underlying structures in their reading and writing—and the differences between literary and more analytic texts—is particularly important for ELL students. The choices we as teachers make in planning have significant implications for how students are positioned as capable readers and writers. This requires attention to our course design and framing: how we scaffold the skills needed, how we help students make connections between their reading and writing, and how we respond to students as they grapple with the challenges in these areas.

Positioning students' expertise in relation to these different language demands in a positive way can help them learn how to contribute both socially and academically. For example, William tracks his students' areas of expertise based on their writing and discussions of texts. He uses this knowledge to pair and group students during peer feedback on writing. A student who is able to generate big ideas may be paired with a student who constructs perfect sentences but with little depth. Or a student who has the ability to use new adjectives creatively after a mini-lesson and analysis of mentor texts might be paired with a student who is struggling in this area. By tracking students' strengths and language abilities, we help students develop their own metacognitive abilities to set goals for future development.

Finally, we can model and explain how readers and writers negotiate various language demands that shift from genre to genre. As we all know, no writer or reader has completely mastered all the genres and contexts for literacy and language learning. We all make errors as we learn and we all bring strengths and areas for growth to the community. Many published writers have discussed this truth, which can help us support students through a more nuanced understanding of what it means to be fluent or proficient as readers and writers in a language.

Meeting the Curricular Challenges: Tips for Supporting ELL Students in Rigorous, Responsive Reading Communities

The following tips build on the discussion in this chapter and remind us of actions we can take to support ELL students in a rigorous, respectful classroom community.

Eliana, district ELL coordinator, offers a list of tips for mainstream teachers:

- Make use of visuals, gestures, and other nonverbal ways to communicate.
- Regularly check for understanding rather than just asking if students have questions.
- Allow and encourage students to use their native language to support their content learning.
- Establish and communicate high standards of rigor to your students, regardless of their English proficiency level. Facilitate honest discussions [with your ELL students about their needs], while also communicating that you are confident in your ability to teach them, and their ability to learn, so that all students can be successful. Set high standards and expectations, and empower students with the skills and knowledge for them to achieve success.
- Build trust. Learn about students' backgrounds and interests. What are the students' goals? Show a personal interest in each student. Have understanding and empathy for students' challenges outside of class. Learn about their different cultural backgrounds and customs.
- Establish relationships with parents. Do not let the language barrier deter this communication. Use a translator as needed. Communicate with parents to let them know of any concerns. Invite parents to contact you; again, use of a translator should be encouraged.
- Be a positive role model by setting an example through your own attitude and behavior. Show students that it's okay to make mistakes by modeling your own learning and error correction. Model a strong positive work ethic and goal setting.

Next Steps: Patience and Passion in Supporting Rigorous Reading Opportunities

Patience. You can help your students develop patience with themselves and also see the possibilities for their work as readers by not needlessly limiting them to truncated versions of classroom learning. No matter what curricular choices you make, your ELL students need a range of opportunities to engage with texts and produce oral and written language. Supporting their reading engagement includes planning opportunities for reading silently, reading orally, and listening to text being read. They also need opportunities to respond to texts orally and in writing. To help students engage fully with these activities, model how readers take on new challenges by taking risks and building on existing resources.

Most important of all, make sure that students have time for sustained and meaningful reading in your classroom. Likewise, students need to write in a multitude of genres. Christina Ortmeier-Hooper's book (2017) in this imprint, *Writing across Culture and Language: Inclusive Strategies for Working with ELL Writers in the ELA Classroom*, describes the length of time it can take ELL student writers to produce a full text and the importance of supporting them as writers. We must demonstrate what is possible in our community of readers so that students know they can expand their reading abilities and identities in sophisticated, savvy ways.

Allowing students choice in *what* and *how* they read texts with a variety of themes, reading levels, and perspectives can also support their identities as readers. Giving students authentic opportunities to write in response to texts, consider mentor texts in different genres (i.e., read like writers), and explore their identities as writers—these are all important to everything students are learning as readers.

Getting Started: Ask Yourself

Questions about Curriculum and the Literacy Community

Our ELL students need us to ask questions about our curriculum that recognize these areas:

- How are we creating cultural and linguistic connections to build on multilingual students' cultural, personal, and community assets?
- How are we paying attention to students' backgrounds and prior knowledge with text selection?
- How are we front-loading to support students in active, cooperative learning contexts with varied purposes?
- How are we providing scaffolding through understanding the multiple language demands of our ELA content?
- How are we pairing reading and writing tasks strategically?
- How are we fostering awareness of reading and writing as separate yet connected?

Passion. This is what we must add to our classrooms as we consider how to support what students bring to the classroom and ask them to be contributing members of our reading communities through active, supported literacy interactions.

> Once we believe in ourselves, we can risk curiosity, wonder, spontaneous delight or any experience that reveals the human spirit.
>
> —e. e. cummings, poet and playwright

Chapter Six

Assessing Teaching and Learning with ELL Students

> "By the time you got to your final position the boat had sailed!"
>
> The boat has sailed . . .? What boat? Oh my God, was there a reference to a boat in the play that I had missed? Wait a minute—wait a minute—a boat sailing away sounds like a good thing. Is he saying I did something good? (Manzano, 2015, p. 236)

In this interaction described in the memoir *Becoming Maria*, the protagonist, a multilingual student, receives an oral assessment of her acting performance from the head of her drama department. The words the teacher uses to critique her performance rely on an idiom that Maria, as an advanced bilingual student, doesn't understand, so she is left unsure of the meaning of her mentor's feedback.

In a way, the mentor is on the right track, as he attempts to give Maria somewhat informal, ongoing feedback to help improve her performance. However, he misses the proverbial boat by not realizing that she doesn't actually understand his feedback. First, he uses language that isn't responsive to Maria's language understandings. Second, because he doesn't realize their lack of communication, he doesn't provide specific input into the desired goal for the next performance. Last, he doesn't encourage her reflection and input into the assessment process.

Consider what might have happened had the conversation started with the director asking the student actor to describe what she noticed about her performance the night before, what questions she was asking herself, or what goals she had developed based on the audience's reaction. Of course, luckily for the rest of us, she eventually goes on to become Maria in *Sesame Street* and in that role worked to help share explicit language and multicultural knowledge with kids all over the United States. Tellingly, though, this event stuck out in Maria's memory as she grappled with disconnects in school and beyond based on language, educational preparation, and gaps in cultural capital.

Given the national conversations about assessment, you may be wondering: how do I assess the practices discussed in earlier chapters? This chapter affirms ways to use assessments productively to communicate high expectations for all students by prioritizing multiple assessments, formative assessment, self-assessment, various authentic assessments, attention to discourses about assessment, and teacher inquiry.

> ***Key Understanding:*** **Language use is contextualized, and assessing proficiency must vary based on context, audience, and mode and in response to a range of factors.**

The Importance of Multiple Assessments

Research shows that ELL students need multiple types of assessments, including self-assessment opportunities and authentic assessments (DelliCarpini, 2009; Pandya, 2011). Assessments can be structured to acknowledge differences between spoken and written language and distinctions between language and content objectives. To support our ELL students, we must pay attention to how language intersects with assessment design and how we develop shared discourses related to assessment with our students.

Based on her experiences supporting mainstream teachers of ELL students, Eliana, the district ELL coordinator, reminds us of the range of feedback and assessment required in good teaching:

> Provide both constructive criticism and positive feedback. Good teaching is teaching students how to learn. Create an environment of learning where students want to know "why" they didn't get it or "how" they got to the answer. Feedback should

be formative as well as summative, and should include self-assessment for students to take ownership of their learning.

Using What We Know about Formative Assessment and Self-Assessment

Applying Key Elements of Formative Assessment

We know that formative assessment is especially crucial for ELL students. Formative assessment is an active, ongoing process throughout a series of events, not an isolated event. NCTE's Task Force on Assessment developed the position statement "Formative Assessment That *Truly* Informs Instruction" (2013), which provides a summary of ten elements found to underpin formative assessment. It:

1. Requires students to take responsibility for their own learning.
2. Communicates clear, specific learning goals.
3. Focuses on goals that represent valuable educational outcomes with applicability beyond the learning context.
4. Identifies the student's current knowledge/skills and the necessary steps for reaching the desired goals.
5. Requires development of plans for attaining the desired goals.
6. Encourages students to self-monitor progress toward the learning goals.
7. Provides examples of learning goals including, when relevant, the specific grading criteria or rubrics that will be used to evaluate the student's work.
8. Provides frequent assessment, including peer and student self-assessment and assessment embedded within learning activities.
9. Includes feedback that is non-evaluative, specific, timely, and related to the learning goals, and that provides opportunities for the student to revise and improve work products and deepen understandings.
10. Promotes metacognition and reflection by students on their work.

We also know that formative assessment can be "on the fly," "planned for interaction," and "curriculum-embedded" (Heritage, 2007, in NCTE Task Force on Assessment, 2013).

How might this position statement support how we assess ELLs in the ELA classroom?

The first point is this: having ELL students in an ELA classroom reminds us of the importance of effective formative assessment for all students and ensures that we articulate high expectations for all while considering ways to differentiate.

Second, NCTE's position statement on formative assessment supports much of what we know about using assessment effectively with ELL students (Brown, 2007; DelliCarpini, 2009; Ferlazzo & Hull-Sypnieski, 2012). While ongoing, purposeful, individualized feedback in a supportive context helps all students, for ELL students we may need to pay extra attention to explaining the rationale and role of formative types of assessment in the ELA classroom, as noted in Table 6.1. We also must attend to the language we use in the assessments. How do principles like these play out in practice? Turning once again to Maja's teaching practices, we can see formative assessment at the center of her work.

Table 6.1. Applying Principles of Formative Assessments to Teaching ELL Students

Principles of Formative Assessment	Application to Teaching ELL Students
1. Requires students to take responsibility for their own learning.	ELL students need to have opportunities to engage actively with learning and to share responsibilities for learning. For example, this means helping ELL students learn how to assess their learning and communicate their strengths and needs to others, while also recognizing potential moments of vulnerability when they may have preparation different from that of their peers.
2. Communicates clear, specific learning goals.	Having clear goals remains critical for work with ELL students; for instance, they should know what kinds of language practices they are working on at a given point. Having specific goals can also mean a slow "unfurling" of goals so that ELL students have opportunities to process the goals.
3. Focuses on goals that represent valuable educational outcomes with applicability beyond the learning context.	Authentic, lifelong learning outcomes support motivation of ELL students, who may become disenfranchised with decontextualized learning that offers no relevance to their language learning goals.
4. Identifies the student's current knowledge/skills and the necessary steps for reaching the desired goals.	New terms are sometimes embedded in different types of assessment, and this is an area of academic language to consider as we support how ELL students understand what is being asked related to assessment. By focusing on assessment as finding out students' current knowledge/skills, we can keep from making assumptions about any given ELL student's reading, writing, and speaking understandings.
5. Requires development of plans for attaining the desired goals.	We may need to help ELL students identify reasonable plans for meeting goals, including helping them prioritize language and content learning goals and set reasonable expectations. Organizational tools and visuals can help students fully understand the goals. We also need to help ELL students plan for ample time to attain goals.
6. Encourages students to self-monitor progress toward the learning goals.	Self-monitoring for ELLs means not only making sure students understand what counts as progress, but also providing examples of how to monitor themselves. Having students help facilitate the monitoring of their progress enables ELL students to take a more active role.
7. Provides examples of learning goals including, when relevant, the specific grading criteria or rubrics that will be used to evaluate the student's work.	We need to make sure ELL students understand the intentions of these assessments as well as why certain criteria may need to be varied or differentiated based on content and language goals. Specific rubrics and criteria can further help communicate how ELL students can challenge themselves.

continued on next page

Table 6.1. Continued

8. Provides frequent assessment, including peer and student self-assessment and assessment embedded within learning activities.	Providing multiple assessments remains key, as we consider the multiple facets of language learning in an ELA classroom. These multiple forms of assessment also provide opportunities for ELL students to apply the language of the assessments in actual situations (e.g., the language needed to conduct a successful peer review of an analytical essay and its effective use of evidence). However, some ELLs may need confidence building and support when giving feedback to peers.
9. Includes feedback that is non-evaluative, specific, timely, and related to the learning goals, and that provides opportunities for the student to revise and improve work products and deepen understandings.	Nonevaluative and timely feedback helps ELLs work on real goal-focused improvement rather than simply copying answers or correcting work without really understanding the reasons why they are making changes. For example, spot-checks of a language objective during a lesson can help you know when to reteach something needed by ELL students.
10. Promotes metacognition and reflection by students on their work.	For ELLs, time to reflect can help them better internalize strengths. It's also especially important to emphasize that genuine ELA learning can entail risk-taking and mistakes that we grow from, especially given the complexity and depth of ELA content.

First, as mentioned in Chapter 3, Maja uses the "Reflective Student Self-Assessment" as an ongoing classroom structure. This self-assessment consists of a narrative that students write on a monthly basis about their work in her class: persuasive and narrative reflections about their grades and community contributions. Students write their reflections based off the Whole-Class Participation Rubric (see p. 45) and Maja's ongoing self-assessment assignment, which she has adapted over time (see p. 125).

Multiple Purposes for Formative Self-Assessments

Maja notes several purposes for having students write these self-assessments, which she uses as part of her ongoing, formative assessment of students:

- *Allows for writing over time:* Reflective self-assessments are monthly assignments that students write as personal narratives.
- *Encourages writing in a narrative genre:* Including this type of writing is important because it provides a moment for students to write beyond the emphases of the Common Core State Standards: argument writing, synthesis, and comparison/contrast—in other words, objective, academic writing.
- *Provides practice in a real-world genre:* This kind of reflective writing also prepares students to write the personal essays they need to perfect by their senior year to be accepted into college.

Principles of Formative Assessment in Maja's Reflective Self-Assessment

This part of the assignment sheet showcases elements described in Table 6.1. Notice how the language of the assessment invites students to communicate their strengths and explicitly signals the audience and structure of the assignment (i.e., the teacher and possibly future college admissions counselors).

Elements of Your Reflective Self-Assessment in Letter Form

Prompt: Choose one or more components from the above rubric and use it (them) to write about yourself—your life as a student, as a human being. Use your writing voice; I want to hear the music of your voice rising from the page.

Writing Voice Components: Diction, syntax, figurative language, details, POV, imagery—unique to you and your experience.

Guidelines:

1. Address me—so be aware of your rhetorical situation.
2. Please type your response (you may find that some excerpts of your self-assessment could be used to cut and paste into your college essays ☺).
3. As you write, be you, be the unapologetic, inimitable, and unique you. Don't hold back. Practice using your own voice, not some generic, stilted academic voice.
4. FEEL FREE TO WIN ME OVER WITH EQUAL AMOUNTS OF ETHOS (gut, experience—sensory details), LOGOS (brain, logic), and PATHOS (heart).
5. Practice writing with Essential Intellectual Traits, implicitly and explicitly. This will benefit you in developing your writing voice and in writing college essays.
6. Remember that you can always submit an addendum with written participation if you feel like being quiet at times.

Some of the criteria on the Reflective Student Self-Assessment rubric are as follows:

The student

- embraces the idea of failure as part of the learning process by articulating confusion and without stigmatizing own or others' mistakes
- asks intellectually curious questions of her- or himself, other students, teacher; uses three levels of questions to share her or his metacognition
- self-starts and offers to engage her- or himself and others in place of the teacher when appropriate
- is consistently focused (no distractions causing discipline issues)
- makes insightful suggestions gently rather than complaining
- engages other students and reminds them gently and amicably to stay on task
- does not dominate by watching her or his airtime [see note on p. 44 about revised phrasing]
- accurately justifies answers; explains assumptions, inferences, and reasoning; supports claims with evidence; draws justifiable conclusions; and accurately interprets textual material

- *Offers an opportunity for personal writing and relationship building:* Writing exclusively academic essays doesn't address the whole student. Personal narratives build relationships between students and teachers so that teachers are able to tailor their instructions to their audience's needs.
- *Helps students understand criteria for community contribution:* Reflective self-assessment begins as a way for students to internalize what it means to be a student who contributes to Maja's classroom community. Students are provided with grading profiles describing an A student, a B student, etc. Then in writing, students examine their performance for each month and document moments that support their claims about how well they are progressing in mastering the rubric.

Encouraging and structuring self-assessment also has the potential to help you assess students' ongoing language understandings. Maja's students are required to assess themselves while using rhetorical understandings of ethos, logos, and pathos in order to address all their needs and successes (see Table 6.2. Using Rhetorical Understandings during Self-Assessment). Maja's assignment refers to students' past knowledge of ethos (gut, experience—sensory details), logos (brain, logic), and pathos (heart). Applying rhetorical understandings during self-assessment requires practical application and an authentic audience. The assignment also provides an opportunity to teach and reinforce academic language (i.e., the rhetorical strategies and their applications).

Table 6.2. Using Rhetorical Understandings during Self-Assessment

	Definition	**Description on Assignment**	**Types of Student Responses**
Ethos	Credibility appeals: relies on author's authority	"gut, experience—sensory details"	· Descriptions of key learning and their individual roles · Phrases such as "I assure you . . ." "digging deeper," or "waiting to pounce"
Pathos	Emotional appeals: appeals to the heart	"heart"	· Descriptions of feelings in class and in response to interactions such as "acceptance," "love," "little uncomfortable," "fears," "blessed" · Phrases such as "I believe . . ." and "I felt . . ."
Logos	Logical appeals: relies on reason	"brain, logic"	· Quotations cited from class or interdisciplinary learning, e.g., response to a specific excerpt or aspect of the discussion · Examples of their moves in class, specific learning targets met · Phrases such as "If they were to . . ." or "cannot be the case" or "For example"

Communicating Explicit High Expectations to All Students

Structuring clear, high expectations for students—and empowering ELL students to engage in ongoing self-assessment—requires us to communicate these expectations to all students through consistent (and early) discussion, written and oral guidelines, and sensitivity to students' understandings of the expectations.

Tips adapted from Maja:

- Communicate expectations from the beginning of the school year and reinforce them every day for a few weeks, then once a week, and finally as you see fit.
- Make sure students understand that you will be supporting them throughout this process.
- Explain (and show explicitly) that you never stigmatize mistakes but view them as opportunities.
- Discuss each expectation and modify it if students need the expectation to be articulated differently. Maja does this when she communicates her high expectations in the Whole-Class Facilitation Rubric for discussion (in Chapter 3).
- Essential: Communicate so that expectations are positively framed, explained clearly and warmly, and are understood by students.

In Practice: Syllabus as a Starting Place for a Respectful Assessment Environment

Key Practices in This Vignette

- Valuing students' contributions
- Offering explicit, rigorous expectations
- Structuring authentic assessment
- Modeling how to assess and understand assessments (over time)

At the beginning of the school year, in addition to her syllabus, Maja hands out her Whole-Class Participation Rubric, which outlines what a student needs to do to be an A or a B student, as well as what a C or a D student looks like. Maja describes how this detailed handout delineates the behaviors students are expected to exhibit to be successful:

> Some of the rules are "acknowledging other students' contribution by name and piggybacking off their contribution," and "pushing back gently on what the other students and the teacher have said."

I introduce these rules gradually because students need time to internalize them. At first we review them every day, and as time goes by, we reflect on them once a week. Also, students are required to write their monthly Reflective Student Self-Assessments in the form of a letter to me in which they can openly voice their concerns regarding the classroom atmosphere, how well they are internalizing the rubric, and how the rubric impacts their grades.

These Reflective Student Self-Assessments are also made to be fun—although students are to advocate for a certain participation grade, which includes respect, they are also allowed to communicate with me informally using metaphors and analogies so that I can better understand how to help them.

Also, this is the best way for my true ELLs to express themselves because often they are reluctant to participate because, as they told me, they have "accents." In other words, when surrounded by native or near-native speakers, ELLs may clam up, so it is up to me to help them slowly leave their shells.

They blossom in small groups, and many of them eventually become comfortable communicating in whole-class discussions. For example, a few years ago, I had an ELL student who had anxiety attacks when communicating in whole-class discussions. He described his crippling anxiety in his Reflective Student Self-Assessments—which were well written, poignant, but also funny. Once I realized he had a sense of humor, I made sure that I shared his jokes and acknowledged his other input effusively. With ELLs, it is important to focus on and acknowledge the content of their contribution and build relationships with them.

Including Multiple, Ongoing Authentic Assessments (versus One-Shot Standardized Assessments)

Now that we've addressed the role of formative and self-assessment as key to ELL student learning, you may be wondering about the role of standardized assessments. You certainly have received testing data meant to inform your teaching, though my advice is to let it inform rather than drive your teaching—especially for ELLs. Our standardized assessments often gloss over the complexity of multilingual student learning in our mainstream classrooms; while they can offer some insights into certain aspects of language understandings, be forewarned that you are often seeing only one aspect of language use being evaluated in a particular format under constrained circumstances.

In "Assessing the English Language Learner (ELL)" (in Lapp & Fisher, 2011), scholars address reliability and validity concerns with using the same standardized assessments for native English speakers and ELL students. They note how official classifications for ELL students can be problematic, because we are all learning English over a lifetime. When nationalized assessments discuss identifying a proficient "English level," it's important to note that there is no consensus about how that level is determined across standardized assessments. In addition, too often these standardized assessments conflate language proficiency and content knowledge (DelliCarpini, 2009), an obvious issue for the accuracy of these measures for ELLs. This discussion of assessments is a whole can of worms on its own, but if you're interested, you're in luck, because Betsy Gilliland and Shannon Pella's *Beyond "Teaching to the Test": Rethinking Accountability and Assessment for English Language Learners*, another volume in the Teaching English Language Learners strand of the Principles in Practice imprint, offers a much deeper discussion of this topic.

The main takeaway that should lead us to focus on multiple authentic assessments rather than one standardized snapshot is that language use is contextualized; proficiency will vary based on context, audience, and mode and in response to a range of factors. To design authentic assessments, we have to consider first what the assessment actually measures.

- Does it measure cultural contexts or experiences? DelliCarpini (2009) describes how sometimes our assessments use imagery or assumptions that are culturally based, like references to a jigsaw puzzle (played by students in some parts of the United States) rather than to Chigora Danda, a popular children's game "played in Zimbabwe but [that] may have roots in India" (p. 117).
- Does the assessment help ELLs make connections between their lives and the curriculum?

DelliCarpini stresses that "one thing that English teachers can focus on is performance-based measures of ELLs on authentic tasks that offer a variety of ways that ELLs can show they are mastering the content" (p. 118). Such authentic assessments or performance-based measures require us to consider assessments that may connect to real-life literacy tasks, genuine audiences, application of (rather than regurgitation of) content, task-based assessments (versus selecting an answer), and student-structured choices (or multiple acceptable routes) to demonstrating understanding.

To design these authentic assessments effectively, we have to make our objectives and criteria visible to ourselves and to our students. Here's where structuring authentic assessments is a way to apply your learning from Chapter 4's focus on the multiple language demands that ELL students face in the range of academic, social, written, and verbal contexts for language use. Identify the language demands inherent in your assessments, such as interactive social language that may need to be modeled for peer review interactions. Make these language-based objectives (and your scaffolds to support students in meeting them) explicit.

Unpacking Discourses of Assessment

Unpacking the discourses of assessment can help ELL students participate effectively in formative and other assessments, especially as they take on responsibility for learning in self- and peer assessments. Just as we may sometimes struggle to get our heads around new institutional assessments, we need to support our ELL students in particular as they navigate assessments. Supporting ELL students' understanding of assessments requires time spent discussing the language and criteria (explaining in both written and oral forms), using visuals and models to increase understanding, allotting sufficient time to explore assessment elements and academic language, and encouraging students' interactions with assessment design.

Maja describes her approach to introducing students to the whole-school rubrics, using gradual unpacking of the rubric criteria:

> We have a few rubrics designed by the English I team or adapted from Common Core and/or College Readiness Standards. Whenever I introduce a rubric, I "unfurl" it over the course of a few weeks, if not months.
>
> For example, our Argument Writing Rubric assesses students on claims, evidence, analysis, syntax, and coherence. However, it is impossible for students to take in all five of these criteria. So when we unfurl claims, students discuss the rubric's descriptions of mastery, emerging mastery, and developing levels, and ask questions or amend the rubric as a class.
>
> It is important for students to understand the assessment tool that will be used to assess their writing, and if they can also contribute to the rubric, they feel empowered because they are given options and a voice with which to adapt the rubric.

Maja's students also use a rubric for peer review and revision.

District ELL Coordinator Eliana confirms this approach, which focuses on providing challenges for ELL students while also clearly modeling how they can achieve the expectations.

> It is important for teachers to differentiate instruction in order to meet the needs of all students, and to appropriately challenge them to their abilities. Teachers should model outcome expectations for students and provide organization tools and rubrics to guide students through the content, rather than simply providing instructions and disseminating information.
>
> The teacher is the facilitator of learning and should provide the necessary scaffolds and tools for students to perform to their abilities and demonstrate knowledge and understanding. [ELL students] in particular should be allowed ample time to process information and to formulate responses. Teachers should make use of visuals, gestures, and other nonverbal ways to communicate in order to make input comprehensible for students at various levels of English language proficiency.

A case in point here is Luis, whom you might remember from an earlier chapter. His teacher realized that she needed more than an oral "yes" from Luis when she asked if he understood something; he needed to demonstrate his understanding in some other way, such as acting it out. Responsive teachers know that sometimes ELL students need to show understanding through nonverbal cues or visuals.

Further, ELL students benefit when teachers model structures to support students' understanding of how to respond to assessments and of which choices are valid. This is where attention to the relationship between what students are reading and what they are being asked to write is especially important, because the texts students read often become mentor texts for how they write. Ann, for example, noted the ways students were able to "see themselves" and connect their own stories to Patricia Reilly Giff's *Wild Girl*, the narrative of a young girl's transition to the United States on a challenging first day of school. The experience of reading and analyzing the story enabled ELL students to respond with their own stories on the state writing exam prompt that asked students to *describe a day when they didn't fit in*, in a narrative format. Some ELL students wrote about their first day of kindergarten, describing a range of experiences—finding a supportive friend, or learning how to communicate with the teacher.

Teacher Inquiry: Sustaining Our Practice through Action Research

Understanding language in our classrooms needs to be an ongoing process due to its complexity and dependence on constantly evolving factors, such as curricular demands and student profiles in any given class. Teacher inquiry—acknowledging what we don't know and exploring in systematic ways how to make positive change—is another way this complexity can enliven our teaching. Nieto (2003) describes how teacher inquiry groups can help sustain us as experienced, ever-evolving educators. Especially as our language understandings develop, our inquiry into classroom practice can help us discover better ways to understand and conduct assessment in our classrooms with ELL students, specifically as we learn to scaffold instruction for the wide range of ELL students and classroom contexts and inquire into the language demands posed by reading different texts and writing in different genres.

For example, when Maja noticed that graphic organizers were sometimes getting in the way of writers' sense of exigency, or passionate, urgent argument, in their AP English writing, especially those who might be considered Generation 1.5 writers, she participated in an action research group to consider how best to support students' authentic writing. Action research helped her explore the challenges of academic writing and how to help her high school writers, who had often been successful as elementary school writers, move into academic writing that requires more than flat, formulaic prose.

As part of her research, Maja analyzed student essays and tracked conversations with students in a teaching journal. The essays she analyzed employed rhetorical devices and schemes and used extended metaphors—even though students weren't familiar with rhetorical schemes. She also conducted a survey to find out which strategies supported and/or got in the way of student learning, and she analyzed samples of successful and less successful student essays, as defined by the College Board. From her investigations, she was able to develop some findings, such as

1. Authentic writing is a vulnerable process—praise and encouragement, especially from peers, helps unlock exigence, or passion.
2. Strategies are tools, not objectives; otherwise, mastering a strategy may take on a life of its own and become a skill separate from the writing goal.
3. Strategies may impose a task-completionist, product-oriented attitude, as opposed to a gradual, deliberate, personalized, exploratory process needed for the college essay.
4. Making constant connections with the real world and personal lives may unlock exigence within.
5. Students need to be given time to "stew" and "marinate" with their own thoughts through freewriting and creative writing, perhaps combining oral participation with written participation.
6. Experiencing writing as a refuge from one's problems affirms writing voice.
7. Allow students to be messy with their thinking.
8. Allow and encourage students to outgrow the strategy.

Action research like Maja's means engaging in a systematic and ongoing research process; it is widely accepted as a systematic process of improving practice in planning, delivering, assessing, and reflecting on lessons. Action research is formative, guiding how we change our lessons, differentiate, approach a lesson from a new angle, or find new ways to form groups—all by responding to the cues our ELL students give us.

Another participant in Maja's action research group, Ruth, describes:

> Action research is iterative—we try over and over, each time in a new way, to help our students master the objectives of a lesson or a unit or a course. We don't say, "Well, they don't seem to comprehend the power of nouns and verbs in writing so we'll just quit trying and let them fill up a page with abstractions, platitudes, and strings of adverbs." Instead, action researchers stay consistent with the objective of teaching students to improve their work. Action research is adaptive: when one approach doesn't work, we adapt to another way of reaching the objective. The objective stays consistent.
>
> Action research **lets students be part of the research process** because their feedback on what and how we teach is plowed right back into the next day's or the next week's plans.

> Action research is **reflective.** The whole point is to look back on what works and what doesn't and start the cycle over again at a level that rests on what we just learned, this time informed by how we nest that learning in a wider **context.**

What we know from research is that action research

- Improves teacher confidence (Godt, 2007)
- Keeps the focus on students in standardized environments (Greene, 2010, 2011)
- Helps teachers learn about English language learners (Sowa, 2009)

A first step is to develop your initial questions and consider data that could help you answer them. As you collect and interpret data, you ask, "So what?," or what are you finding that can help improve your practice (Mills, 2007)? Chapter 7 includes additional resources to support teacher inquiry, and professional development groups often encourage teacher inquiry and reflection, such as the National Writing Project, which provides online resources and locally run summer institutes and inservice programs for schools and institutions.

What is most useful for us as teachers of multilingual students is that action researchers engage in ongoing reflection: Is your research question still answerable and worth answering? Are your data collection techniques catching the kind of data you want and filtering out the kind of data you don't (Mills, 2007, p. 148)? How can you develop an action research plan based on what you are learning about your students and then plan next steps: "Based on what I have learned from this investigation, what should I do now?" (p. 155)? Ortmeier-Hooper's *Writing across Culture and Language* (2017), for example, offers methods for using diagnostic writing and assignments. These can function as initial formative "data" to inform next steps in your classroom, just as teachers like Ann use surveys to learn about their ELL students and plan instruction.

Next Steps: Assessing Teaching and Learning with ELL Students

Unfortunately, our standardized testing environment in the United States complicates how we learn about our ELL students, as well as contributes to a need to think critically about who is and isn't labeled "ELL" and what that means in our classrooms. What we *can* do is advocate for multiple, authentic assessments—working to explain to others how this kind of assessment better serves us and our ELL students than a one-size-fits-all assessment that offers only a brief snapshot of complicated language proficiencies.

Getting Started: Ask Yourself

Questions about Assessment:

- What types and varieties of assessment do you use?
- How do you use self-assessments?
- How do you use formative assessment?
- How do you use standardized test data? What are its limits?
- What discourses of assessment do you share with students?
- How do your assessments match your goals for language learning?
- As a teacher, what questions are you interested in pursuing to improve your practice?

Chapter Seven

Finding Resources and Collaborating with Others

"I just don't know what to do with all these students who don't speak English," a teacher groans in the teacher's lounge one day. Other teachers sitting around agree. "Let's face it—it's hard to keep up standards in your class when a bunch of students in there just don't understand." Another adds, "And the real problem is that their parents just aren't involved."

Imagine this conversation taking place about the new or growing population of ELL students at your school. You've been reading this book and now wonder how to communicate with these colleagues what you now know about language in a multilingual ELA classroom.

"Great," you might be thinking. "Now I have a bunch of new ideas and questions related to a responsive approach that focuses on respect and rigor. What's next?"

I know from my work with inservice and preservice teachers that it's difficult to translate new ideas immediately to classroom practice. One way to start, though, is with questions: either the ones I offer here or the ones that arise for you based in your own context:

- How do I put ideas into action in a meaningful way?
- How do I get support when there is limited time?
- When empowered with new language understandings to explore or apply, how do I shift a negative school culture around an issue? What *should* I do if I hear a colleague talk about how the real problem with ELLs is that their parents aren't involved?
- Perhaps even most important, how do I best communicate with stakeholders beyond my classroom door, especially students' families?

Asking questions is an excellent starting place to help us collaborate with others as we seek to understand how language works in our specific contexts. Starting with questions can help us pay attention to the larger community of stakeholders without making assumptions. This chapter addresses how we can communicate with other community members, such as other teachers, parents or guardians, and administrators. First, the chapter describes tips to help mainstream teachers collaborate with other school stakeholders, such as ESL or resource teachers, as well as request further professional development related to linguistic diversity. The chapter then describes professional development resources that the teacher-friendly annotated bibliography found at the end of the book builds on, listing important professional organizations, books, articles, websites, and video links to support mainstream ELA teachers.

***Key Understanding:* Supporting ELL students in responsive classrooms requires ongoing collaboration around key questions and community building through welcoming communication.**

The Opportunities for Collaboration and Community Building

Paying close attention to how we use language in English teaching clearly provides a myriad of benefits. Not only can it help us interact more effectively with a wide range of students, but it also helps us support the reading, writing, and speaking skills necessary for twenty-first-century success. Additionally, linguistic and cultural awareness enable native English speakers to understand key ELA concepts as well as ways to interact in an increasingly diverse world. To fully reap these benefits, I've found that communicating with others can help support my teaching and the teaching of inservice and preservice teachers. But where do we start?

Educating ELL students is a whole-school responsibility (Soltero, 2011). Ideally, schools acknowledge this responsibility by, for instance, having a diversity action plan that addresses issues of hiring and staffing and developing curricular ways for all students to experience linguistic and cultural diversity. Considering how we support ELL students and their families allows us to support better community engagement and develop more effective collaborations within our schools.

Communicating with the Community: Get On Board with Stakeholders

Here are some tips to help you collaborate with other key stakeholders, including ESL or resource teachers, parents or guardians, and administrators.

How Your School Leaders Can Support You

Identify Current Professional Development Options

First, identify the leaders who can and will support you! Do you have access to specific resources, such as ELL family liaisons or dedicated resource people for the school or district? School leaders who want to support teachers will encourage professional learning communities and provide support for teachers to collaborate with others. Common ways to provide support include

- Release time
- Common prep time
- Opportunities for curricular mapping
- Structures to support cross-curricular observations and peer collaboration

If these supports are not in place, you might suggest that school leaders provide support through on-demand seminars or books for group study related to ways of supporting ELL learners (see the end of this chapter and the annotated bibliography for more ideas).

Assess Overall School Environment

You also can encourage school leaders to work along with you to give voice to ELL students within the overall school environment. The students themselves can help you answer the following question: *Is our school a welcoming environment?* Some schools have ELL students (and families or other stakeholders) rate their experiences at the school, which can give important information about (1) transitions between ELL and mainstream classes, (2) divisions and connections between groups and/or classes, and (3) useful areas for future professional development. Additionally, surveys or ratings can help schools determine ways to improve their communication with families and students, such as consideration of particular groups' communication needs in the school environment. For instance, some schools have found that a whole-school "no Spanish rule" (see Soltero, 2011) is demeaning to multilingual students. A survey can help a school avoid or change such a counterproductive policy. On the flip side, a survey might also reveal deeply held beliefs by families—such as that it would be best for English learning if their children don't use other languages at school or at home—and could provide information to shape further educational exchange between home and school.

Identifying School and District Resources

- Does your district have an ELL coordinator?
- Does your district have a family or school liaison?
- Who develops professional development for your department?
- Are there funding avenues for conference attendance (like NCTE's Annual Convention) or other professional development resources?
- Does your district have a diversity action plan? If so, are ELL students included?
- Are there supports in place for continuing language support in mainstream classrooms?
- Is your current approach to language learning *additive* or *subtractive*?

Note: Here are the basics of the two primary language learning approaches (see Soltero, 2011, p. 70, for additional examples):

- *Additive:* Goal is bilingualism or biliteracy; long-term; multicultural
- *Subtractive:* Goal is monolingualism or monoliteracy; short-term; monocultural

Address Language Myths in Current Environment

As you work to identify the current resources and atmosphere in your context, determine whether there are whole-school myths or assumptions you need to take into account. How, for example, would you answer these questions:

- Are there cross-school myths that need to be addressed? (For example, is there a general belief in the "no Spanish [or other non-English language]" rule, or the myth that students will become fluent in English only if students aren't allowed to speak other languages in the school?)
- Are there assumptions about parental or familial involvement? (For example, is there an assumption that ELL families don't value school?)
- Are there misunderstandings about the kinds of and approaches to language supports in the school? (For example, do teachers and/or administrators feel language supports should end after students leave the "language learning classes"?)

If your answer is "yes" to any of these questions, these are areas that could inform future professional development.

How to Connect with Families

Understand Baseline Information about ELL Students

"Learn about your students, their families, and the communities they represent," recommend Jiménez et al. (2011, p. 143). It's important to understand the diversity of ELLs in the school and classroom in terms of a number of factors:

- Class
- Race and ethnicity
- Educational attainment (in English and in other languages)
- Geographic
- Cultural

At the very least, we need to consider the following about our ELL students' communities:

- Understand the "overview" history of their group in United States
- Know some elements of that group's cultural distinctiveness and contributions to US society

If your school demographic consists of only one or two ethnic or cultural populations, this information may be fairly easy to obtain and share among faculty members. In schools where students come from multiple backgrounds, consider some techniques that schools have used for professional development:

- Neighborhood van tour by experienced school or community members to describe where students come from
- Demographic breakdowns and research split among faculty members

On a personal level, responsive teachers often do the following:

- Know the names of family members
- Inquire about family members (by name) regularly

Tips for Communicating High Expectations for Students

- Display students' work (multilingual work included).
- Establish consistent communication with families.
- Encourage literacy in multiple languages.
- Recognize achievement (social and academic) throughout school setting.

Engage Families by Extending Invitations

School systems need to move beyond a monolithic view of the kinds of supports they should offer families. They need to include multiple perspectives and approaches to family participation, which include inviting families to engage with the school community in a variety of ways.

Here are key questions to consider: What do we identify as family participation or engagement? What are our assumed definitions of "traditional" engagement? Are we open to more "nontraditional" forms of engagement?

If the word on the street at your school is that "the problem is the parents," be sure to question that statement (Valdés, 1996, p. 191). For example, Zentella (2005) notes, "Latino parents are often blamed for the educational failures of their children. . . . Parents are accused of not helping with homework or the learning of English, not attending school parent-teacher meetings, and not reading to children or providing children with books" (p. 13). These accusations are often a result of misunderstandings or rigid definitions of what it means to be an engaged parent or family member. That's why it's important to note that conceptions of "parental involvement" can be culturally specific. In fact, some parents may not be aware of avenues for communicating with teachers. This doesn't mean they don't value education. Some parents who want to be involved may struggle to interpret written notices in English. (See Steven Alvarez's *Community Literacies* en Confianza for additional resources.)

A Question to Consider: Does our school create a welcoming environment for families?

Something as small as the way the school's main office is perceived as welcoming or unwelcoming can affect family involvement. In some cultures, approaching office staff may not be the norm. For instance, some parents of ELL students may be intimidated by busy front office workers or disconcerted by the need to sign in with security guards or show identification (Soltero, 2011).

Sometimes families need an explicit invitation to participate and even to share their resources and knowledge with the school community. Note that there may be complexity even in relation to "what counts as being smart" (Zentella, 2005) in a community. It's important to avoid taking a deficit perspective, especially when we don't know the intimate details of our students' family lives.

Communicating with Families: Tips from Eliana, District ELL Coordinator

From her experiences as ELL district coordinator, Eliana encourages teachers to work on developing trusting relationships:

- *Engage parents in identifying and prioritizing needs for the [ELL] program by developing trusting relationships between the school and community.* The more parents are involved in the development and implementation of program components that support their students, the more invested they will be in the overall success of the program.
- *Communicate to parents that their contributions and input are valuable to the school.* Work to identify and capitalize on the strengths of [ELL] parents, and to leverage those strengths to create an environment of mutual respect and a common goal of advocacy on behalf of the students. You may need to attempt many different strategies to engage parents before you find something that works for your specific population.

Don't give up. Keep trying to make those valuable connections between the school and families. Find out:

- What countries your families come from
- Where your ELL students were born
- What languages they speak (possibly several languages)
- The educational background of families and the type of school system in their countries

If any of your ELLs are migrants, refugees, or students with limited or interrupted formal education, **be careful to NEVER** ask about documentation or immigration status. Other actions you can take include learning about and celebrating the special events or holidays that are important to your students, inviting parents to the classroom to share their traditions, and connecting families with a contact person who speaks their language to assist with the enrollment and registration process.

Family Conferences and Beyond

Teacher-parent (or family) conferences can be an important way to open up lines of communication (Valdés, 1996). Sometimes language abilities will emerge during family conferences, and linguistically responsive teachers will plan for this possibility. Their comments focus on the positive effects of multilingualism, rather than assuming that non-English-language abilities will surface as problems.

In Practice: Maja's Ways of Communicating with Families

Key Practices in This Vignette

- Valuing family contributions
- Creating positive connections
- Expressing openness to communication in multiple ways
- Acknowledging family assets

I keep in touch with my students' families through email and phone calls whenever possible. If the parents don't have email, I call. If the phone number is disconnected, which is common in neighborhood schools, I call the parents' work. If we don't have their work number on file, the school sends a letter.

Generally, I find it most useful to get in touch with my students' families during the first week of school. My first assignment for which students receive credit so that every student starts with an A is to have my students ask their parents/guardians to send me an email with a particular subject line and specific information such as cell number, work number, and their concerns. In this way, I gain a great deal of information about my students' families: their use of email, literacy, technology access, etc.

No matter how I contact the families, it is always important to make a phone call or send an email that is entirely complimentary. Because we're extremely busy, we teachers tend to initiate contact when an issue arises, but it is paramount that we contact the families if something good and positive occurs. This type of communication is a powerful tool for getting parents involved, especially the parents of students who have discipline issues.

As for my Gen 1.5s and ELLs, their parents may often not speak fluent English, so infrequently I need a translator; most of the time, I use my ESL training to talk to the parents by using key words because most parents know some English.

Another way to communicate with the families of my students is through the Parent Portal, which is part of our online gradebook. Also, there is an app called Remind, which is designed for texting communication between teachers, students, and parents. It is used to remind students of assignments as well as to encourage students to ask questions of their teacher through safe text messaging transparent for their parents.

Next Steps: Planning for the Future

After reading this book, you may decide that you want to request further professional development related to linguistic diversity. This book ends with an annotated bibliography that includes important professional organizations, books, articles, websites, and video links that support mainstream ELA teachers. The starred resources are special recommendations from Eliana, based on her expertise in structuring professional development for mainstream content area teachers.

Professional Development Options

- Suggest a book or article study group with colleagues (see descriptions in the annotated bibliography for ideas).
- Consider a partnership with a local university, library, or center.
- Attend conferences or presentations.
- Ask for school-wide professional development.
- Plan to collaborate with bilingual or ELL teachers.
- Join a teacher inquiry or action research group.

Getting Started: Ask Yourself

What Are My Next Steps?

- What questions do I want to pursue?
- Who can I collaborate with?
- What methods do I want to try out?
- What additional resources do I need?

Annotated Bibliography

Articles

Brozek, Elizabeth, and Debra Duckworth.
"Supporting English Language Learners through Technology."
Educator's Voice 4 (2011): 10–15.
https://www.nysut.org/~/media/Files/NYSUT/Resources/2011/March/Educators%20Voice%204%20Technology/edvoiceIV_1103.pdf

With all of the twenty-first-century tools we have today, it's not hard to find ways to extend ELL students' academic language. ESL teachers Elizabeth Brozek and Debra Duckworth acknowledge in this article that English language learners often acquire basic interpersonal communication skills (BICS) before they develop cognitive academic language proficiency (CALP). Since students may be hesitant to use academic language in a classroom setting, an effective method you can use to ease them into these higher-order thinking processes is to incorporate technology into the ways you promote understanding. Through the use of interactive whiteboards, document cameras, video-creation software, social networking, and more, you can provide ELLs with a safe, comfortable, and inviting environment to demonstrate their progress.

Hickey, Pamela J.
"Lingua Anglia: Bridging Language and Learners."
English Journal 105.1: (2015), 102–4.

With the proliferating labels for students learning English, have you ever wondered which one is most appropriate and culturally sensitive? This article clarifies the distinctions between the many names given to students learning English, focusing on how they affect students' sense of self-worth. Hickey argues that teachers need to consider how they are labeling students to avoid creating implied limitations or biases, describing how the terms *emergent bilingual* and *multilingual learner* promote the viewpoint that students have a wealth of linguistic history and cultural experiences and create opportunities for them to share their unique understanding of language with the rest of the class.

Lacina, Jan.
"Technology in the Classroom: Promoting Language Acquisitions: Technology and English Language Learners."
Childhood Education 81.2 (2004): 113–15.

We know there are many benefits to using technology in the classroom, but discussions of incorporating technology rarely focus on how technology can specifically aid ELLs. With ideas based on constructivist learning theory, Lacina explores uses of technology that can help English learners connect content to language in meaningful ways. By providing specific resources ready for classroom use and responses from teachers who have integrated technology into lessons in various ways, she helps all teachers, from elementary to secondary level, find strategies to motivate students using online tools.

Books

Freeman, Yvonne S., and David E. Freeman.
ESL/EFL Teaching: Principles for Success.
Portsmouth, NH: Heinemann, 1998.

The question we always seem to be grappling with is how we can translate the best principles for teaching English learners into actual classroom practice. This book provides a clear transition between principle and practice by examining eight distinct theories that teachers should consider while planning instruction. Not only does it delve into the underlying meanings of each principle, but it also gives related lesson and project ideas, as well as examples from real teachers in the field who have succeeded using these methods.

Ortmeier-Hooper, Christina.

The ELL Writer: Moving beyond Basics in the Secondary Classroom.

New York: Teachers College Press, 2013.

Since oral language development often precedes written language, ELLs face a particular challenge in our classrooms when given writing assignments. Ortmeier-Hooper discusses her experiences through interviews with six different ELL students, sharing their stories and development in school-based writing. These six case studies provide insight into the diverse perspectives represented in an increasing number of classrooms today, demonstrating that all teachers need to be prepared to teach ELL writers.

Vogt, MaryEllen, Jana Echevarría, and Deborah Short.

The SIOP Model for Teaching English-Language Arts to English Learners.

Boston: Pearson, 2010.

Creating detailed lesson plans may seem like a tedious task, but your ELL students benefit greatly from your advanced planning. As a follow-up to the book *Making Content Comprehensible for English Learners: The SIOP Model* (Echevarría, Vogt, & Short, 2008), this book demonstrates classroom applications of the eight-step and thirty-feature SIOP model. This planning method utilizes both content and language objectives to engage ELLs in meaningful and differentiated instruction. The authors also offer a plethora of ideas for modifying lessons and activities so that ELL students feel better supported in their content and language understandings.

*Starred resources are those recommended by Eliana, a district ELL coordinator.

Topical Resources

Using the SIOP Model to Develop Academic Language and Objectives

Consider these resources for example lesson plans with both content and language objectives:

- *Short, Deborah, and Jana Echevarría. *Developing Academic Language with the SIOP Model.* Boston: Pearson, 2015.
- *Echevarría, Jana, MaryEllen Vogt, and Deborah Short. *Making Content Comprehensible for English Learners: The SIOP Model.* 2nd ed. Boston: Allyn and Bacon, 2004.

Understanding Language Knowledge, Variation, and Myths

Consider these lessons related to language variation and academic writing:

- Brown, David West. *In Other Words: Lessons on Grammar, Code-Switching, and Academic Writing.* Portsmouth, NH: Heinemann, 2009.

Consider these quick reads to understand common misconceptions about language and language variety:

- Johnson, David. *How Myths about Language Affect Education: What Every Teacher Should Know.* Ann Arbor: University of Michigan Press, 2008.
- Samway, Katharine Daview, & Denise McKeon. *Myths and Realities: Best Practices for Language Minority Students.* Portsmouth, NH: Heinemann, 1999.

Consider this text's useful survey for formative assessment of students' language knowledge (see pages 123–24):

- Aguilar, Cynthia Mata, Danling Fu, and Carol Jago. "English Language Learners in the Classroom." In Kylene Beers, Robert E. Probst, and Linda Rief (Eds.), *Adolescent Literacy: Turning Promise into Practice* (pp. 105–25). Portsmouth: Heinemann, 2007.

Inquiring into Classroom Practice through Action Research

Use this guide to develop a teacher action research project or a project in a departmental or school inquiry group:

- Mills, Geoffrey E. (2011). ***Action Research: A Guide for the Teacher Researcher*** (4th ed.). Boston: Pearson, 2011.

Designing Responsive School-Wide or Departmental Approaches

Check out these resources for more in-depth reading as you consider collaborative, school-wide, or departmental approaches, such as communicating with administrators or across your school:

- DeCapua, Andrea, and Ann C. Wintergerst. ***Crossing Cultures in the Language Classroom.*** Ann Arbor: University of Michigan Press, 2004.
- Soltero, Sonia W. ***Schoolwide Approaches to Educating ELLs: Creating Linguistically and Culturally Responsive K–12 Schools.*** Portsmouth, NH: Heinemann, 2011.
- Vásquez, Anete, Angela L. Hansen, and Philip C. Smith. ***Teaching Language Arts to English Language Learners*** (2nd ed.). New York: Routledge, 2013.

Websites

***"Challenges for ELLs in Content Area Learning."**
everythingESL.net www.everythingesl.net/inservices/challenges_ells_content_area_l_65322.php

Outlines a long list of challenges that ELL students face when reading literature in English.

***¡Colorin Colorado!**
www.colorincolorado.org/

Provides all kinds of great resources and suggestions! Describes stages of language acquisition, stages of cultural accommodation, and much more.

***"Developing Programs for English Language Learners: Glossary."**
U.S. Department of Education
www2.ed.gov/about/offices/list/ocr/ell/glossary.html

Provides definitions of ELL/bilingual terminology.

Equity for ELLs
Sarah Ottow and Alyssa Ottow
https://sites.google.com/site/writersesl/home

Includes reading lists, presentations, and handouts on a blog by two practicing elementary teachers focused on providing equal educational opportunities for ELL students.

Facing History and Ourselves
https://www.facinghistory.org/

Provides helpful resources for interdisciplinary lesson ideas related to themes of fostering civil discourse, dealing with prejudice, and promoting cultural understandings; includes sample texts, teaching methods, standards-aligned lessons, and other resources.

***"Learning Disability or Language Development Issue?"**
www.everythingesl.net/inservices/special_education.php

Helps teachers distinguish between learning disabilities and language acquisition issues.

"A Map of Languages in the United States"
The Modern Language Association Language Map
https://apps.mla.org/map_main

Provides searchable information about language and culture with interactive maps and tables that can be tailored to target demographics and regions.

"Sheltered Instruction Observation Protocol."
Center for Applied Linguistics
www.cal.org/siop

Lays out the fundamentals of the SIOP model of sheltered language instruction.

"Understanding Language MOOCs Featured in Stanford Graduate School of Education Article."
Understanding Language
Graduate School of Education
Stanford University
http://ell.stanford.edu/content/understanding-language-moocs-featured-stanford-graduate-school-education-article

Provides an article with links to other articles and resources about MOOCs developed by the Understanding Language Initiative as professional development for teachers.

***"WIDA's 2012 Amplification of the ELD Standards."**
English Language Development (ELD) Standards, WIDA
www.wida.us/standards/eld.aspx

Includes links to a free download of WIDA standards and an explanation of the theoretical framework.

NCTE Resources

- ***English Language Learners: A Research Policy Brief***
  http://www.ncte.org/library/NCTEFiles/Resources/PolicyResearch/ELLResearchBrief.pdf
- ***Language Learners in the English Classroom*** (2007) Douglas Fisher, Carol Rothenberg, and Nancy Frey
  https://secure.ncte.org/store/language-learners-in-the-english-classroom
- Conference on English Education's Position Statement ***Supporting Linguistically and Culturally Diverse Learners in English Education*** focuses on the education of diverse learners through inquiry activities related to language use.
  http://www.ncte.org/cee/positions/diverselearnersinee
- ***Text Messages*** podcasts by Jennifer Buehler on ReadWriteThink.org, e.g., "Latino Literature for Teens"
  www.readwritethink.org/parent-afterschool-resources/podcast-episodes/latino-literature-teens-30972.html
- Other books in the Teaching English Language Learners strand of the Principles in Practice imprint:

  Beyond "Teaching to the Test": Rethinking Accountability and Assessment of English Language Learners (2017) Betsy Gilliland and Shannon Pella
  https://secure.ncte.org/store/beyond-teaching-to-the-test

  Community Literacies* en Confianza: *Learning from Bilingual After-School Programs (2017) Steven Alvarez
  https://secure.ncte.org/store/community-literacies-en-confianza

  Writing across Culture and Language: Inclusive Strategies for Working with ELL Writers in the ELA Classroom (2017) Christina Ortmeier-Hooper
  https://secure.ncte.org/store/writing-across-culture-and-language

Centers and Professional Organizations

CAL: Center for Applied Linguistics, www.cal.org

NABE: National Association for Bilingual Education, www.nabe.org

NAME: National Association for Multicultural Education, www.nameorg.org

NCELA: National Clearinghouse for English Language Acquisition, www.ncela.us

NCTE: National Council of Teachers of English, www.ncte.org

NHLRC: National Heritage Language Resource Center, http://international.ucla.edu/nhlrc

TESOL: Teachers of English to Speakers of Other Languages (international association), www.tesol.org

References

Adger, C. T., Snow, C. E., & Christian, D. (Eds.) (2002). *What teachers need to know about language*. McHenry, IL: Delta Systems/Washington, DC: Center for Applied Linguistics.

Alvarez, S. (2017). *Community literacies* en confianza: *Learning from after-school bilingual programs*. Urbana, IL: National Council of Teachers of English.

Ariza, E. N. W. (2010). *Not for ESOL teachers: What every classroom teacher needs to know about the linguistically, culturally, and ethnically diverse student* (2nd ed.). Boston: Allyn and Bacon.

Bear, C., & McEvoy, J. (2015). In California schools, thousands of English language learners getting stuck, *KQED News*. Retrieved from http://ww2.kqed.org/news/2015/06/09/in-california-schools-thousands-of-english-language-learners-getting-stuck

Boyd, F. B., Ariail, M., Williams, R., Jocson, K., Sachs, G. T., McNeal, K., . . . Meyer, T. (2006). Real teaching for real diversity: Preparing English language arts teachers for 21st-century classrooms. *English Education, 38*(4), 329–50.

Brooks, M. D. (2015). "It's like a script": Long-term English Learners' experiences with and ideas about academic reading. *Research in the Teaching of English, 49*(4), 383–406.

Brown, D. W. (2009). *In other words: Lessons on grammar, code-switching, and academic writing*. Portsmouth, NH: Heinemann.

Brown, H. D. (2007). *Principles of language learning and teaching* (5th ed.). White Plains, NY: Pearson Longman.

Case, A. F. (2015). Beyond the language barrier: Opening spaces for ELL/non-ELL interaction. *Research in the Teaching of English, 49*(4), 361–82.

Charity Hudley, A. H., & Mallinson, C. (2011). *Understanding English language variation in U.S. Schools*. New York: Teachers College Press.

Cummins, J. (2000). *Language, power, and pedagogy: Bilingual children in the crossfire*. Buffalo, NY: Multilingual Matters.

Curzan, A. (2014). *Fixing English: Prescriptivism and language history*. Cambridge, UK: Cambridge University Press.

Daniels, H. (1994). *Literature circles: Voice and choice in the student-centered classroom*. Portland, ME: Stenhouse.

De Oliveira, L. C. & Silva, T. J. (2013). *L2 writing in secondary classrooms: Student experiences, academic issues, and teacher education*. New York: Routledge.

DeCapua, A., & Marshall, H. W. (2010a). Serving ELLs with limited or interrupted education: Intervention that works. *TESOL Journal, 1*(1), 49–70. doi:10.5054/tj.2010.214878

DeCapua, A., & Marshall, H. W. (2010b). Students with limited or interrupted formal education in US classrooms. *Urban Review, 42*(2), 159–73. doi:10.1007/s11256-009-0128-z

DeCapua, A., & Marshall, H. W. (2011). Reaching ELLs at risk: Instruction for students with limited or interrupted formal education. *Preventing School Failure, 55*(1), 35–41.

DeCapua, A., & Wintergerst, A. C. (2004). *Crossing cultures in the language classroom*. Ann Arbor: University of Michigan Press.

DelliCarpini, M. (2009). Success with ELLs: Authentic assessment for ELLs in the ELA classroom. *English Journal, 98*(5), 116–19.

Delpit, L. D. (1995). *Other people's children: Cultural conflict in the classroom*. New York: New Press.

Echevarría, J., Vogt, M., & Short, D. (2004). *Making content comprehensible for English learners: The SIOP model* (2nd ed.). Boston: Pearson/Allyn and Bacon.

Echevarría, J., Vogt, M., & Short, D. (2008). *Making content comprehensible for English learners: The SIOP model* (3rd ed.). Boston: Pearson/Allyn and Bacon.

Ellis, N. C., & Larsen-Freeman, D. (2006). Language emergence: Implications for applied linguistics—Introduction to the special issue. *Applied Linguistics, 27*(4), 558–89.

Enright, K. A. (2013). Adolescent writers and academic trajectories: Situating L2 writing in the content areas. In L. C. de Oliveira & T. J. Silva

(Eds.), *L2 writing in secondary classrooms: Student experiences, academic issues, and teacher education.* (pp. 27–43). New York: Routledge.

Faltis, C., & Coulter, C. (2008). *Teaching English learners and immigrant students in secondary schools.* Upper Saddle River, NJ: Pearson/Merrill Prentice Hall.

Faltis, C., & Wolfe, P. M. (1999). *So much to say: Adolescents, bilingualism, and ESL in the secondary school.* New York: Teachers College Press.

Fecho, B. (2004). *"Is this English?": Race, language, and culture in the classroom.* New York: Teachers College Press.

Ferlazzo, L., & Hull Sypnieski, K. (2012). The ESL/ELL teacher's survival guide: Ready-to-use strategies, tools, and activities for teaching all levels. San Francisco: Jossey-Bass. Retrieved from http://proxy.cc.uic.edu/login?url=http://site.ebrary.com/lib/uic/docDetail.action?docID=10593139

Fisher, M. T. (2005). From the coffee house to the school house: The promise and potential of spoken word poetry in school contexts. *English Education, 37*(2), 115–31.

Freeman, Y. S., & Freeman, D. E. (1998). *ESL/EFL teaching: Principles for success.* Portsmouth, NH: Heinemann.

Fu, D. (2007). Teaching writing to English language learners. In T. Newkirk & R. Kent (Eds.), *Teaching the neglected "R": Rethinking writing instruction in secondary classrooms* (pp. 225–42). Portsmouth, NH: Heinemann.

Gebhard, M., Harman, R., & Seger, W. (2007). Reclaiming recess: Learning the language of persuasion. *Language Arts, 84*(5), 419–30.

Gilliland, Betsy, and Pella, S. (2017). *Beyond "teaching to the test": Rethinking accountability and assessment for English language learners.* Urbana, IL: National Council of Teachers of English.

Godley, A. J., Carpenter, B. D., & Werner, C. A. (2007). "I'll speak in proper slang": Language ideologies in a daily editing activity. *Reading Research Quarterly, 42*(1), 100–31.

Godt, P. T. (2007). Leadership in reading: Action research: Putting teachers into the driver's seat when planning classroom research studies. *Illinois Reading Council Journal, 35*(3), 39 43.

Goldenberg, C. N., & Coleman, R. (2010). *Promoting academic achievement among English learners: A guide to the research.* Thousand Oaks, CA: Corwin.

Greene, K. (2010). Research for the classroom: From reluctance to results: A veteran teacher embraces research. *English Journal, 99*(3), 91–94.

Greene, K. (2011). Research for the classroom: The power of reflective writing. *English Journal, 100*(4), 90–93.

Harklau, L. (1999). The ESL learning environment in secondary school. In C. J. Faltis & P. M. Wolfe (Eds.), *So much to say: Adolescents, bilingualism, and ESL in the secondary school* (pp. 42–60). New York: Teachers College Press.

Heritage, M. (2007). Formative assessment: What do teachers need to know and do? *Phi Delta Kappan, 89*(2), 140–45.

Hickey, P. J. (2015). Lingua anglia: Bridging language and learners. *English Journal, 105*(1), 102–4.

Hollins, E. R., & Torres Guzman, M. (2006). Research on preparing teachers for diverse populations. In M. Cochran-Smith & K. M. Zeichner (Eds.), *Studying teacher education: The report of the AERA panel on research and teacher education* (pp. 477–548). Mahwah, NJ: Lawrence Erlbaum.

Hyland, N. E. (2005). Being a good teacher of black students? White teachers and unintentional racism. *Curriculum Inquiry, 35*(4), 429–59.

Jimenez, R. T., Rose, B. C., Cole, M. W., & Flushman, T. R. (2011). English language learners: Language and relationships. In D. Lapp & D. Fisher (Eds.), *Handbook of research on teaching the English language arts* (3rd ed., pp. 139–44). New York: Routledge.

Johnson, D. (2008). *How myths about language affect education: What every teacher should know.* Ann Arbor: University of Michigan Press.

Krashen, S. D., & Terrell, T. D. (1983). *The natural approach: Language acquisition in the classroom.* Hayward, CA: Alemany Press.

Kucer, S. B., Silva, C., & Delgado-Larocco, E. L. (1995). *Curricular conversations: Themes in multilingual and monolingual classrooms.* York, ME: Stenhouse.

Lapp, D., & Fisher, D. (2011). *Handbook of research on teaching the English language arts* (3rd ed.). New York: Routledge.

Lee, S. J. (2005). *Up against whiteness: Race, school, and immigrant youth*. New York: Teachers College Press.

Lippi-Green, R. (2012). *English with an accent: Language, ideology and discrimination in the United States* (2nd ed.). New York: Routledge.

Lucas, T., & Villegas, A. M. (2011). A framework for preparing linguistically responsive teachers. In T. Lucas (Ed.), *Teacher preparation for linguistically diverse classrooms: A resource for teacher educators* (pp. 55–72). New York: Routledge.

Manzano, S. (2015). *Becoming Maria: Love and chaos in the South Bronx*. New York: Scholastic Press.

McBee Orzulak, M. J. (2006). Reviving empathy and imagination: Arts integration enlivens teaching and learning. *English Journal, 96*(1), 79–83.

McBee Orzulak, M. J. (2012). Beyond what "sounds right": Reframing grammar instruction. *Language Arts Journal of Michigan, 27*(2), 21–24.

McBee Orzulak, M. J. (2013). Gatekeepers and guides: Preparing future writing teachers to negotiate standard language ideology. *Teaching/Writing: The Journal of Writing Teacher Education, 2*(1), 12–21.

McBee Orzulak, M. J. (2015). Disinviting deficit ideologies: Beyond "that's standard," "that's racist," and "that's your mother tongue." *Research in the Teaching of English, 50*(2), 176–98.

McBride, J. (1996). *The color of water: A black man's tribute to his white mother*. New York: Riverhead Books.

Melnick, S. L., & Zeichner, K. M. (1998). Teacher education's responsibility to address diversity issues: Enhancing institutional capacity. *Theory Into Practice, 37*(2), 88–95.

Mills, G. E. (2007). *Action research: A guide for the teacher researcher* (3rd ed.). Upper Saddle River, NJ: Pearson Merrill/Prentice Hall.

Moll, L. C., & Gonzalez, N. (1994). Lessons from research with language-minority children. *Journal of Reading Behavior, 24*(4), 439–56.

Musetti, B., Salas, S., & Perez, T. (2009). Success with ELLs: Working for and with Latino/Latina immigrant newcomers in the English language arts classroom. *English Journal, 99*(2), 95–97.

National Council of Teachers of English, Conference on English Education (CEE). (2005). Supporting linguistically and culturally diverse learners in English education. CEE Position Statement. Retrieved from http://www.ncte.org/cee/positions/diverselearnersinee

National Council of Teachers of English, ELL Task Force. (2006). NCTE position paper on the role of English teachers in educating English language learners (ELLs). Retrieved from http://www.ncte.org/positions/statements/teacherseducatingell

National Council of Teachers of English, Task Force on Assessment. (2013). Formative assessment that *truly* informs instruction. Retrieved from http://www.ncte.org/positions/statements/formative-assessment/formative-assessment_full

Nieto, S. (1999). *The light in their eyes: Creating multicultural learning communities*. New York: Teachers College Press.

Nieto, S. (2000). *Affirming diversity: The sociopolitical context of multicultural education* (3rd ed.). New York: Longman.

Nieto, S. (2003). *What keeps teachers going?* New York: Teachers College Press.

Noddings, N. (2005). *The challenge to care in schools: An alternative approach to education* (2nd ed.). New York: Teachers College Press.

Ogbu, J. U., & Simons, H. D. (1998). Voluntary and involuntary minorities: A cultural-ecological theory of school performance with some implications for education. *Anthropology & Education Quarterly, 29*(2), 155–88.

Ortmeier-Hooper, C. (2013a). *The ELL writer: Moving beyond basics in the secondary classroom*. New York: Teachers College Press.

Ortmeier-Hooper, C. (2013b). "She doesn't know who I am": The case of a refugee L2 writer in a high school English language arts classroom. In L. C. de Oliveira & T. J. Silva (Eds.), *L2 writing in secondary classrooms: Student experiences, academic issues, and teacher education* (pp. 9–26). New York: Routledge.

Ortmeier-Hooper, C. (2017). *Writing across culture and language: Inclusive strategies for working with*

ELL writers in the ELA classroom. Urbana, IL: National Council of Teachers of English.

Pandya, J. Z. (2011). *Overtested: How high-stakes accountability fails English language learners.* New York: Teachers College Press.

Reid, S. E. (2002). *Book bridges for ESL students: Using young adult and children's literature to teach ESL.* Lanham, MD.: Scarecrow Press.

Rex, L. A., & Schiller, L. (2009). *Using discourse analysis to improve classroom interaction.* New York: Routledge.

Roser, N., Martínez, M., & Wood, K. (2011). Students' literary responses. In D. Lapp & D. Fisher (Eds.), *Handbook of research on teaching the English language arts* (3rd ed., pp. 264–70). New York: Routledge.

Schleppegrell, M. J. (2004). *The language of schooling: A functional linguistics perspective.* Mahwah, NJ: Lawrence Erlbaum.

Schleppegrell, M. J., & Go, A. L. (2007). Analyzing the writing of English learners. *Language Arts, 84*(6), 529–38.

Scott, J. C., Straker, D. Y., & Katz, L. (2009). *Affirming students' right to their own language: Bridging language policies and pedagogical practices.* New York: Routledge/Urbana, IL: National Council of Teachers of English.

Soltero, S. W. (2011). *Schoolwide approaches to educating ELLs: Creating linguistically and culturally responsive K–12 schools.* Portsmouth, NH: Heinemann.

Sowa, P. A. (2009). Understanding our learners and developing reflective practice: Conducting action research with English language learners. *Teaching and Teacher Education, 25*(8), 1026–32.

Valdés, G. (1996). *Con respeto: Bridging the distances between culturally diverse families and schools: An ethnographic portrait.* New York: Teachers College Press.

Valenzuela, A. (1999). *Subtractive schooling: U.S.-Mexican youth and the politics of caring.* Albany: State University of New York Press.

Van Sluys, K. (2005). *What if and why? Literacy invitations for multilingual classrooms.* Portsmouth, NH: Heinemann.

Vásquez, A., Hansen, A. L., & Smith, P. C. (2013). *Teaching language arts to English language learners* (2nd ed.). New York: Routledge.

Vogt, M., Echevarría, J., & Short, D. (2010). *The SIOP model for teaching English-language arts to English learners.* Boston: Pearson.

Wiley, T. G., & Lukes, M. (1996). English-only and Standard English ideologies in the U.S. *TESOL Quarterly, 30*(3), 511–35.

Wilhelm, J. D. (2012). *Improving comprehension with think-aloud strategies: Modeling what good readers do* (Rev. and updated ed.). New York: Scholastic.

Wolfram, W. (1998). Language ideology and dialect: Understanding the Oakland Ebonics controversy. *Journal of English Linguistics, 26*(2), 108–21.

Young, V. A., Barrett, R., Young-Rivera, Y'S., & Lovejoy, K. B. (2014). *Other people's English: Code-meshing, code-switching, and African American literacy.* New York: Teachers College Press.

Zentella, A. C. (2005). *Building on strength: Language and literacy in Latino families and communities.* New York: Teachers College Press/Covina: California Association for Bilingual Education.

Index

Author

Melinda J. McBee Orzulak is an associate professor at Bradley University in Peoria, Illinois, where she teaches future teachers and serves as the English education coordinator. Her research focuses on equity and language in English language arts teaching. Before working as an English teacher educator in Illinois and Michigan, she taught high school English, writing, and humanities. McBee Orzulak's research is inspired by her teaching in multiple high-need schools, where she engaged with ongoing teacher conversations about equity, English, and meeting the needs of ELL students. Her work has appeared in multiple venues, including the journals *English Journal*, *Research in the Teaching of English*, and *English Education*, as well as in the edited volume *Teaching English Language Arts to English Language Learners*. She is a coauthor of *Taking Initiative on Writing: A Guide for Instructional Leaders*. She can be reached at mmcbeeorzulak@bradley.edu.

This book was typeset in Janson Text and BotonBQ by
Barbara Frazier.

Typefaces used on the cover include American Typewriter,
Frutiger, and Formata.

The book was printed on 60-lb. White Offset paper
by Versa Press, Inc.